Revenue Capture Scorecard®

Revenue Capture Scorecard®

How to Grow Your Business Using
Metrics and a Planned Process

By

Paul R. DiModica

ISBN 10 Digit: 1-933598-90-5
ISBN 13 Digit: 978-1-933598-90-1

Published by Johnson & Hunter, Inc.

Trademarks

Contents

iii

Preface

To grow a business in today's economic environment, CEOs and executive management teams need a planned process based on a defined strategy which uses metrics and is executed in a timely manner. This information will help management team members make the necessary decisions to proactively adjust business operations so they reach the stated corporate objectives.

Growing your firm's top-line revenues is not a simplistic business model that just focuses on what the sales team is doing or a sales distribution model (retail, wholesale, Internet, etc.) that is operationally efficient.

Instead, growing your revenue must be a coordinated event where specific departments work in tandem as an integrated effort to move the revenue capture needle.

Not managing your business model in this way is high risk.

Focusing on the sales process as the primary path to business growth is a limiting model that actually reduces business growth. The sales team (or distribution process) you use does not operate individually but is the operational driver of a collective group that is concentrated on the same goals.

If you are a growth-directed firm, to increase your business success, you must integrate *sales*, *marketing*, *strategy*, and *financial management* models into one outbound Revenue Capture Scorecard.

Each of these four perspectives has a symbiotic relationship with the other. When managed separately, as silos, they cause the other perspectives to fail and the ultimate objective of revenue growth will not be accomplished.

Some leadership teams believe sales capture improvement cures all. While having an increase in sales can make this true… it is also true that money hides mistakes. Thus revenue capture must be a coordinated approach linked to operational profitability—which is the purpose of a Revenue Capture Scorecard.

When attempting to build a business model that is scalable and replicable, the executive management team must concentrate on department integration, metric knowledge, best practices, and a planned process with clearly defined corporate objectives.

Revenue growth is also tied to the executive teams' business knowledge of why prospects buy and why they do not buy. Once these essentials are understood, the information must be integrated into a broader framework of business drivers that accelerate business growth.

No business department operates in a vacuum. Just having a low price, the best widget, a beautiful website, a committed social network, stellar service department, or a great sales team does not mean more prospects will buy—because your strategy could be wrong. Having a great, inbound lead-generation program managed by your marketing department does not mean that revenues will increase—because your pricing and financial models could force the targeted buyer to hesitate. Moreover, having a world-renowned brand does not automatically generate revenue—because brand recognition does not mean brand acquisition.

In today's global economy, being an industry innovator of products or professional services means nothing if you can't market and sell your offerings against the "me-too" competitors that steal your intellectual property or mass-produce your product in a Third World country at a fraction of your cost.

The secret to obtaining revenue growth consistently in any economic environment is using a planned process that is metric and meta-data driven where the whole company works in tandem using a defined methodology and knowledge base to drive revenue as a company, in totality.

In this book, we give you a defined model using the Revenue Capture Scorecard as a process to grow your business. But for the sales, marketing, strategy, and finance departments to be correctly integrated together in a Revenue Capture Scorecard framework and have their metrics correctly measured, you must also look at best practices and the objectives of these departments to help maximize your prospective integration. We also give you best practices and thought leadership for each department's operational approach to help you maximize your performance so it can be successfully integrated and linked to your Revenue Capture Scorecard.

Metric management does more than just measure the success or failure of assigned objectives. It also allows your operational department executives to better understand the business responsibilities needed to manage their areas of control more efficiently.

Executives must also know how to improve their decision process to adapt their operational capabilities based on their departments' changing success criteria. Business success happens when the collection of metrics provides greater knowledge _and_ the executive management team executes based on that knowledge.

Chapter 1

Overview and History

My Exposure to the Balanced Scorecard

Prior to forming my own companies, I was Vice President of Strategic Development for Renaissance Worldwide, a public company headquartered in Boston, Massachusetts. (Renaissance was originally called The Registry, Inc., which purchased the consulting firm Renaissance Solutions Inc., owned by David Norton. Norton co-authored the book *The Balanced Scorecard* with Robert Kaplan.) Renaissance Solutions focused on providing consulting services using the Balanced Scorecard as a framework. The Balanced Scorecard management methodology is a dominant strategy used worldwide by Global 1000 companies. To better reflect its corporate strategic management direction, The Registry changed its name to Renaissance

Worldwide and centered their business model on the Balanced Scorecard approach and becoming a worldwide consulting and technology-implementation advisement firm. As the senior corporate strategy executive working directly for the CEO, I was cognizant of this business process.

After observing the Balanced Scorecard's original practice, I identified what I believe is an operational gap in its design and ultimate deployment. What I discovered was that the Balanced Scorecard is a strong management tool for large multi-national companies, such as Ford, IBM, American Express, and others that have well-established and mature business success models, revenue growth year over year that is incremental, and a corporate financial momentum that is solidified.

But what about growth-directed companies that want to build a sustainable revenue-capture model and have growth greater than 5% year after year? Alternatively, what about market-dominant players that want to act small and be more agile in the market so they can adapt to the Internet-speed model of purchases?

Although I recommend the Balanced Scorecard concept to any company that is comfortable with its business model being mature and is looking to build a business process that is focused on operational and systems excellence only—based on my observations, the Balanced Scorecard process holds back the agility and ability of small- to medium-sized businesses and large company divisions to adjust their business strategy as needed.

More than ever, agility is a key performance indicator to a company's success in today's worldwide economy. (Of course, this is just my opinion.)

While advising hundreds of public and private companies of all sizes, I have witnessed many firms that have detailed operational metrics on product and service production and delivery, and operational cost controls; and yet, they function with minimal knowledge and metrics of their revenue-capture process.

The Balanced Scorecard process is a *pre-Internet* business tool. The Internet has changed business success models and has forced companies to learn how to adapt, become agile, or fail. Having strong operational and production systems are important, but without having a replicable and scalable revenue-capture system in place (or one that is agile), their value diminishes over time.

Dictionary.com defines *agility* as the power of moving quickly and easily; and … the ability to think and draw conclusions quickly.

The Revenue Capture Scorecard is a *post-Internet* business agility management tool focused on building a buyer strategy that is linked to revenue capture success. It aligns sales, marketing, strategy, and financial management simultaneously into a planned, outbound, revenue-capture process that can help you adjust your business model as needed to proactively make quick decisions.

Has Amazon.com excelled because of the worldwide distribution and delivery methodology it developed? Of course, but without Amazon.com's understanding of how to make customers buy (revenue capture) and the metrics that drive customers to buy, its multi-billion dollar investment in computerized distribution centers would be wasted assets.

The Revenue Capture Scorecard is *different*.

The Revenue Capture Scorecard is not a rigid company framework that forces department compliance to some corporate objective. Instead, it is a framework that is fluid. A living, breathing, GPS, leadership platform that makes executive leaders agile in their decision process and guides them to needed action steps that should be implemented now to increase corporate revenue capture based on current market activities.

The purpose of using a Revenue Capture Scorecard is to develop specific qualitative action steps that are measured for each of these four areas (sales, marketing, strategy, and financial management) to help executive teams create a visual tool of performance to grow and adapt their business as it happens or as quickly as it can be measured—not just manage it after the fact.

Revenue capture models are never stagnant. As customers' buying characteristics change so too does the methodology to capture their business.

Through the Revenue Capture Scorecard, the four revenue-driver areas are linked together for true revenue-capture success. The alignment and linkage of these areas is the key foundation to make your revenue capture a managed process that works correctly while also giving you the agility and ability to make adjustments in your business model as changes happen.

Revenue capture does not operate in a silo. Sales cannot go up if marketing does not generate qualified leads and prospects. Revenues will not improve if your strategy has you selling blue shoes to a red shoe market. If your pricing is wrong, it does not matter how well your sales team members are trained or how intuitive your website navigation is—growth will be stagnate.

To grow revenues, you must use a coordinated process, where all of the moving gears and levers work in tandem, and where your revenue machine does not overwhelm ongoing adjustments in your capture process as they happen. Today, more than ever, revenue capture is an "in the moment" success model.

Often when the Balanced Scorecard is compared to the traditional Management by Objective (MBO) approach, it is described as measuring today against tomorrow versus the MBO approach of measuring what you do today against what you did yesterday.

Waiting quarterly for detailed knowledge of your firm's revenue capture model means that you are reactive to what you did yesterday, not proactive on what you can do today or tomorrow.

This retrospection and reactive approach does not afford you the opportunity to adjust your business's ability to sell when your prospects are buying—and that is a primary variance between the Revenue Capture Scorecard and the Balanced Scorecard.

Chapter 2

Determine Your Potential for Growth

Defining and Measuring Your Current Potential for Business Growth

The first step to building an integrated revenue-capture process is to take a non-emotional 360° assessment of your business's potential to generate revenue while hitting corporate objectives. Revenue-capture success depends on your firm's ability to effectively align its departments so that it is a focused process. Alignment can only happen when you have set a benchmark to measure by.

While working with hundreds of executive teams since 2001, we have identified over 300 business metrics that can be measured directly or indirectly across a company's infrastructure that are tied to revenue-capture success.

Assessing and measuring your current potential for
success helps establish a standard of measurement
that you can use to make necessary adjustments in
your business model to move forward. Once a
holistic assessment of your entire business model's
potential has been completed and department
success potential analyzed, you are then able to set
up Key Performance Indicators (KPIs) that can
define and measure your organizational progress
from where you are to where you want to be. All
KPIs must be quantifiable and measurable and tied
to the executive team's strategic direction.

Our management consulting advisers typically
discover that sales, marketing, strategy, and
financial management departments are not aligned
as a revenue-producing team and the executives
have limited best practice knowledge and KPI
metric management for these areas independently—
even in companies with accelerated year-over-year
growth. This is often due to the management team's
preoccupation with its department's day-to-day
operational issues and its lack of research into
industry best practices.

In many corporate transformations where growth
becomes the new mantra, we often find change
management discussions to be inhibited due to team
members' lack of experience and knowledge on

how to achieve a strategic adjustment involving both the thought process and execution of change.

Generating a strategic shift in operational success is more than managing your metrics and KPIs better. The process involves a holistic cultural adjustment in the team's thinking and execution process on how to grow a business—an adjustment that must trickle down from the boardroom to the mailroom.

Recently, at one of the largest tradeshows in North America, I had the opportunity to chat with the senior vice president of a Fortune 50 company who was responsible for all tradeshow management. With an annual tradeshow budget, counting labor cost, that exceeded $500 million USD, it was surprising to hear that he and his team did not track cost-per-lead by show attended or by product or service offering.

Without this knowledge, how could they know if their marketing, strategy, sales, or financial models and expenditures made sense or were generating a tradeshow return on investment (ROI) or if their departments were working in tandem (or in conflict) to help increase year-over-year sales and profits?

This lack of expenditure tracking and ROI knowledge is surprising—but not uncommon in both large and small companies.

A growth-directed firm seeking to build a scalable and replicable revenue-capture process must establish a baseline of its current process by completing a 360° assessment of the firm's revenue-producing departments, the departments' relationship with each other, and the use of best practice approaches.

In order to be successful, this process of completing a revenue-capture success analysis must be free of personal perceptions, ego, and biased opinion. The objective of this diagnostic audit of your business potential for success is to identify revenue-capture gaps in your growth model that can be adjusted and amended.

Once you have completed this assessment, you will have a foundation to start from, build on, and measure against.

Moving From an Entrepreneurial Managed Business Process to a Professionally Managed Business Process

The Revenue Capture Scorecard is not just a "fix-the-problem" business success tool; it is also a GPS guidance system for firms seeking performance guidelines on how to scale and replicate current operating models and entrepreneurial processes.

We often work with successful, privately owned companies seeking even greater success. Many of the principals, through their own sheer determination, core competencies, and positional strength, have pulled their business forward and built an enterprise that by any definition is successful. Yet, many times, we find these firms managing their business organization process entrepreneurially.

Deploying an entrepreneurially managed business process is not to say that the management team is unprofessional, nor that their revenues are not growing or that they are not profitable. The difference between an entrepreneurially managed business process and a professionally managed business process is that entrepreneurially managed business processes often do not have a structured model of growth or metrics that are planned, tracked, measured, and managed.

Without these elements, it is difficult for a company to scale and replicate. Using an entrepreneurially managed business process minimizes your business valuation for an exit strategy, equity funding, or business forward momentum after the principals have left.

The success of your business growth is not based on the quality or construction details of the product or service you sell but rather on the strength of the revenue-capture process you deploy.

Does your product or service offering have to be competitive? Yes, of course.

But in today's worldwide market, where the Internet has made all buying options visible, many times quality products and service capabilities are simply good enough.

If your business is technical or engineering-driven or you are a founding entrepreneur who has created a new widget or unique service and you are emotionally tied to your firm's offerings, this truth might make you uncomfortable and intellectually you may disregard it. But building an innovation-driven business based on attaining the premier brand or quality position in your market niche without having an equal or better revenue-capture process in place is a wasted investment and thought process.

Companies like Eastman Kodak, Pan Am Airlines, Blockbuster, Polaroid, Yahoo, Xerox, and Sears were innovative pioneers in their respected industries … and yet … where are they today?

Innovation must be linked to a metric-measurement of business success.

The world is littered with examples of dead companies that over-engineered their offerings or had early strategic and brand market success but lost their command positions because competitors' revenue capture models outperformed them.

In today's world of 24/7 instant access, social network media, mobile communication and Internet connection, buyers are always in an ongoing stage of information collection, information fatigue, and sometimes over-information dissemination. The influx of product and service information and subsequent detailed analysis has led to an incorrect belief by buyers (and sellers) that the buyer knows how to buy correctly.

The truism that affects all companies trying to grow revenue is that information consumption by the targeted buyer does not mean information accuracy.

To be a growth-directed firm that is consistently leveraging this flow of information and to build a company that is scalable and replicable, you need to have a defined revenue-capture process that is measureable and premeditated, where the information you absorb becomes useful tools that you can implement.

History shows that firms that focus equally on revenue-capture frameworks, brand marketing, and innovation become sustainable companies.

Jeff Bezos founded Amazon.com in July 1994. Lore has it that when selecting the company's name, Bezos wanted it to begin with the letter A so it would show up early in an alphabetic search. Instead of focusing on the company's name and brand, he concentrated his efforts on building an innovative model and revenue-capture distribution framework driven by metrics that are scalable. Today, Amazon.com is mightily feared by retailers, distributors, and wholesalers of products that can be shipped by postal mail or United Parcel Service (UPS).

In the book *"Great by Choice,"* Jim Collins discusses how companies that statistically have year-over-year growth success in all economic markets are firms that use a planned process that is metric driven.

To build a professionally managed business model, both privately owned and publically managed firms must operate from a detailed metric model and a best practice position where all departments work in tandem and are focused on a success strategy to achieve revenue capture.

To build a sustainable success model, you must utilize four linked elements. They are:

1. You must understand that revenue capture is a company responsibility.

2. You must market and sell the results your offering creates or offers your target prospect.

3. You must manage your business by metrics and KPIs.

4. You must link your strategy to your revenue-capture process.

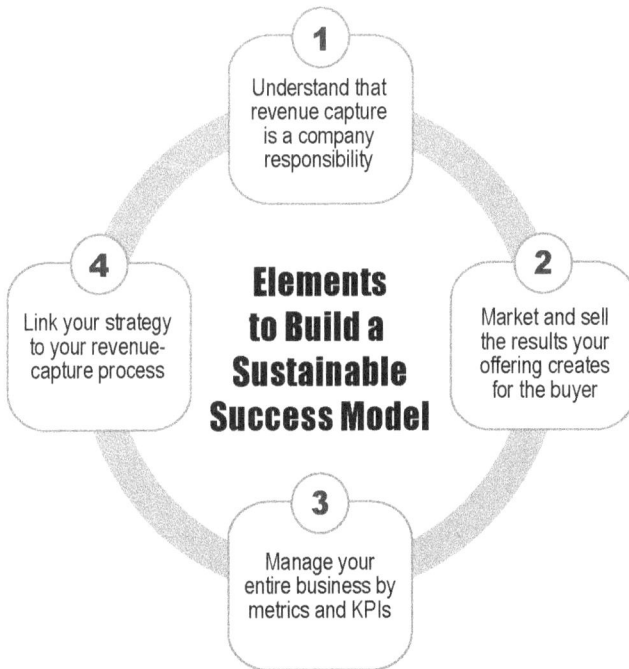

1

Understand that revenue capture is a company responsibility

4

Link your strategy to your revenue-capture process

Elements to Build a Sustainable Success Model

2

Market and sell the results your offering creates for the buyer

3

Manage your entire business by metrics and KPIs

By implementing these four drivers, then and only then can you establish a sustainable and scalable revenue-capture process for your business.

It's All About Being Agile ... In The Now

The Revenue Capture Scorecard focuses on what you did today, as it happens, and points you to what you need to do tomorrow to hit your stated strategic objectives.

By tracking and adjusting specific weekly and/or monthly key performance drivers as they develop, you maximize your potential to grow top-line revenues. Small changes in your Revenue Capture Scorecard metrics can produce huge improvements in your revenue-capture success.

The Revenue Capture Scorecard is all about being agile ... in the now.

Implementing a Revenue Capture Scorecard helps executive teams visually monitor their departments' individual performances and synergistic potential to build an integrated revenue-capture program.

Utilizing Revenue Capture Scorecards drives companies to success by guiding teams through a thought leadership process that is rule-based and focuses on objectives that can be implemented, measured, and adjusted as needed.

How the Revenue Capture Scorecard Areas Were Selected

The foundational concept of the Balanced Scorecard is that management must align the four perspectives of Customers, Learning and Growth, Financial, and Internal Business Processes to experience and build revenue growth. As stated in Chapter 1, the Balanced Scorecard has tremendous merit when used by well-established, large conglomerates that seek to increase their business infrastructure and management performance.

But to use the Balanced Scorecard as a tool to build a growth strategy and increase revenue growth in today's global economy is suspect at best for large companies and fails to address the needs of small- to medium-sized companies on how to build a replicable and scalable revenue-capture program that is measurable and premeditated.

In the business market space:

> PR is not revenue.
>
> Marketing is not revenue.
>
> Operations is not revenue.
>
> Advertising is not revenue.
>
> Branding is not revenue.
>
> Development is not revenue.
>
> *Revenue* is revenue.

Growing a business is all about *revenue*.

Yes, growth can be a complicated model and there are many divergent strategies that require multiple change striations to succeed, but in its simplest form—for companies of any size—revenue growth can be broken down into four straightforward tenets:

1. Who am I selling to?

2. How will I reach them?

3. How will I sell them?

4. How will I make a profit?

These four, when linked together, create the Revenue Capture Scorecard in its basic form.

```
┌─────────────────┐              ┌─────────────────┐
│    Strategy     │    ──────▶   │   Marketing     │
│   Perspective   │              │   Perspective   │
│                 │              │                 │
│ Who am I selling to? │         │ How will I reach them? │
└─────────────────┘              └─────────────────┘

        ▲          Business Growth          │
        │                                    ▼

┌─────────────────┐              ┌─────────────────┐
│    Financial    │              │     Sales       │
│   Management    │    ◀──────   │   Perspective   │
│   Perspective   │              │                 │
│ How will I make a profit? │    │ How will I sell them? │
└─────────────────┘              └─────────────────┘
```

From my experience as a sales, marketing, strategy, and operations executive in different companies (some managed by the Balanced Scorecard model), and as a company founder, I know that having great development, engineering departments, and operations means nothing if you cannot generate revenue based on deploying a focused strategy.

Over the years, while assessing the analytical concepts and success gaps of the Balanced Scorecard, I created a new process called the "Revenue Capture Scorecard®."

19

Why Sales, Marketing, Strategy, and Finance Are the Basis of the Revenue Capture Scorecard

Business success (aka business *growth*) is centered on revenue capture. Product and service delivery, manufacturing quality, corporate customer care, and operation development are important—but without sufficient revenues for your firm to grow, their need is minimalized.

Think about it. The value of your business is not based on the quality of the construction details of the product you sell or on the strength of your delivery capabilities of the service you supply; not over the long-term. The true value of your business is the based on the strength of your sales-and-marketing distribution model and its ability to capture revenue.

Has your firm ever lost a large deal or customer to a competitor that either out-marketed or out-sold you—or both? Has your firm ever launched a new customer offering that was diligently designed, technically superior, appropriately priced, and expertly supported—and no one bought?

Since your value must exceed your price, for sales operations to be effective, your marketing, strategy, and financial models must work in tandem to drive the sales process synergistically. This is the only way to confirm that the value of your product or service exceeds its price.

Lead and Lag Departments

All departments, regardless of their focus, can be divided into a lead or lag revenue center. Like traditional line and staff position allocation, departments either directly or indirectly contribute to revenue capture. But when a lag department is the primary focus of executive management as the key business differentiator for the company, revenue growth can be jeopardized.

Concentrating corporate resources on technical, engineering, or operations capabilities—as the primary department drivers to increase revenue— never works in the long-term.

Long-term, scalable, revenue-growth opportunities only happen when sales, strategy, and marketing distribution equals or *exceeds* the quality of your product and service offerings and the price you sell at.

Everything that is sold, including airplanes, clothing, food, software, tractors, architectural design, professional services, warehouse storage, legal services, automobiles, and manufacturing require detailed sales and marketing planning and metrics that are linked to a pricing and strategy process that is designed to induce your targeted buyers to buy. Just because you have the "best" service or product does not mean your revenue will go up; not unless your sales and marketing strategy is correctly identified and deployed.

In 1985, the Coca-Cola Company, one of the dominant beverage players in the world, decided to replace Coke with a new formula. After spending tens of millions of dollars on technical design, ingredient formulation, and operational delivery setup, they created a different beverage called "New Coke." On April 23, 1985, at a large press conference held in New York City, they launched New Coke. From the first day, nothing went right. Existing customers complained aggressively, sending hundreds of thousands of letters and messages to the CEO demanding he bring back the original Coke formula.

This innovative product failed and was a complete disaster for Coca-Cola because executive management did not link its strategy model with its sales and marketing approach.

Just because you create something unique does not mean buyers will buy it. Did New Coke fail because it did not taste good? No. Pre-testing analysis of the

New Coke flavor showed a high acceptance among consumers.

New Coke failed because it was incorrectly marketed and sold.

To grow your business, you *must* focus on setting up and linking—in detail—your strategy, sales, marketing, and financial models to your revenue-capture objectives as an integrated process to help you reach your revenue goals and to help minimize failure.

Joint Linkage = Joint Accountability

What makes the Revenue Capture Scorecard successful is that it reinforces that revenue capture is a company responsibility, i.e., there is joint accountability, and that departments must work in tandem to help the company become growth-directed.

The foundational design of the Revenue Capture Scorecard focuses on unlocking organizational structures that hinder collective team success and promotes joint accountability amongst the sales, marketing, strategy, and finance departments. Through the scorecard's design, strategic discipline by the executive team becomes a group formation process where all managers are linked to each other's key performance indicators (KPIs) and the corporate revenue goal. By creating a model of continuous improvement, where revenue capture is broken down into measured metrics, the designated departments become integrated together as one team.

Using the integrated Revenue Capture Scorecard helps executives identify the utility value of information as a strategy success tool. Through the use of this utility, managers quickly learn that making small adjustments in their business model linkage, based on their KPIs, can drive huge improvements in their department's success.

This process of *linked accountability* drives revenue performance. Small changes in your business model can create huge changes in revenue growth.

"Management is all about managing in the short term, while developing the plans for the long term."
--Jack Welch

Chapter 3

Strategy Perspective

Defining and Measuring the Strategy Perspective

Wikipedia defines *strategy* as a plan of action designed to achieve a specific goal. Strategy is all about gaining (or being prepared to gain) a position of advantage over adversaries or best exploiting emerging possibilities.

The word *strategy* is derived from the Greek word *strategos;* its operational foundational structure comes from military planning. During the early expansion of the Roman Empire, military legions were positioned based on the objectives of the Roman Senate's initiatives to defend and expand the geography they controlled. Military legions were pre-positioned as both passive enemy (competitor) inhibitors and as outbound territory expansion enablers. Even the language of strategic planning implies military origins. Words like *tactics, logistics, command, control,* and *objectives* permeate C-level discussions.

But simply put, *strategy* is identifying the specific pathway to reach stated objectives. When done correctly, strategy is a GPS system that guides you and your executive team on the action steps you need to take, or not take. Like a military campaign, your stated strategy should give marching orders to your operational army of what to do, how to defend, and how to move forward.

Without having a defined business model strategy, not only will your Revenue Capture Scorecard fail, but your business will also miss its growth objectives. Managing sales, marketing, and financial models without any coherent linkage to your strategy minimizes your success potential and makes your metrics and benchmark data isolated reference points with no relevance.

The pivotal question is: do you have a written corporate strategy that identifies your company's stated goals?

Identify Why Your Offering Sells Or Doesn't Sell

For corporate strategy to be effective, it must go further and be a documented action plan that is broken into identifiable steps directing executive management (and team members) on what steps they and their operating departments need to implement immediately to maintain corporate alignment. It should include:

- Who you are.

- Who you want to be.

- How this model will help you exploit your business success opportunities.

Med Yones, an international financier and thought leader who predicted the U.S. financial crisis, once said: "Sustaining high business performance is a product of continuous strategic alignment." Building your strategy perspective and then aligning it with the rest of your business model is the first step to successfully creating revenue growth.

What are the key attributes needed to build a corporate strategy—one that creates a blueprint and department linkage for the rest of your Revenue Capture Scorecard's perspectives (sales, marketing and finance)?

27

Strategy development is defined as a process that outlines the organization's goals and objectives now and for the future. It reflects the organization's stated intentions of what executive management wants to accomplish. When building your strategy perspective (which ultimately will be measured), there are eight questions that must be answered. These eight questions, which are divided into two stages, might seem simplistic on the surface, but the answers help create a framework that can be adjusted and managed to drive performance and make your competition irrelevant.

Stage One—Knowledge Needed to Grow Your Business

To build a strategy perspective for your Revenue Capture Scorecard that can be measured and managed, you must answer these questions:

1. Why do prospects buy from me?

2. Why do prospects <u>not</u> buy from me?

3. How do I create value that prospects will believe?

As a company principal, you have a fiduciary responsibility to know the correct answers to these questions and how this information should be used as revenue-capture tools for all of the departments to operate correctly. Don't just leave it up to the sales, marketing, and strategy departments to draw conclusions based on their assumptions. When answering these questions, you cannot give generic responses. They must be specific and granular. Do not guess. If you don't know, then you must do research to determine the exact answers.

Oftentimes when we pepper management teams with these questions, they usually respond with assumptions, hunches, and unsubstantiated observations.

Strategy that is successful and scalable must be data driven. Management assumptions wear on business success.

Once you have data that is correct, you need to integrate the answers into your marketing message, your sales process, your customer service and operational departments, and your overall corporate strategy and brand positioning to help create an integrated revenue-capture program.

Stage Two—Knowledge Needed to Understand Why Your Prospects Buy

There are five primary reasons why prospects buy. That's it. Only five! Buyers in both business-to-business (B2B) and business-to-consumer (B2C) are driven by these five questions, both consciously and subconsciously:

1. How does your product or service increase income for the buyer (business-to-business market)?

2. How does your product or service decrease expenses for the buyer (business-to-business market)?

3. How does your product or service manage business risks or consequences for the buyer (business-to-business market)?

4. How does your product or service make the buyer more agile in their business process (business-to-business market)?

5. How does your product or service make the buyer feel good (business-to-consumer markets)?

By working through these five questions and combining your answers with the answers from the three questions in stage one, you are ready to build a strategy that is sustainable, measurable, and can be linked to other scorecard perspectives.

The answers to these eight questions hold the foundational knowledge you need to build your company strategy into a sustainable year-over-year growth model and help create identified metrics that should be measured and appropriately managed.

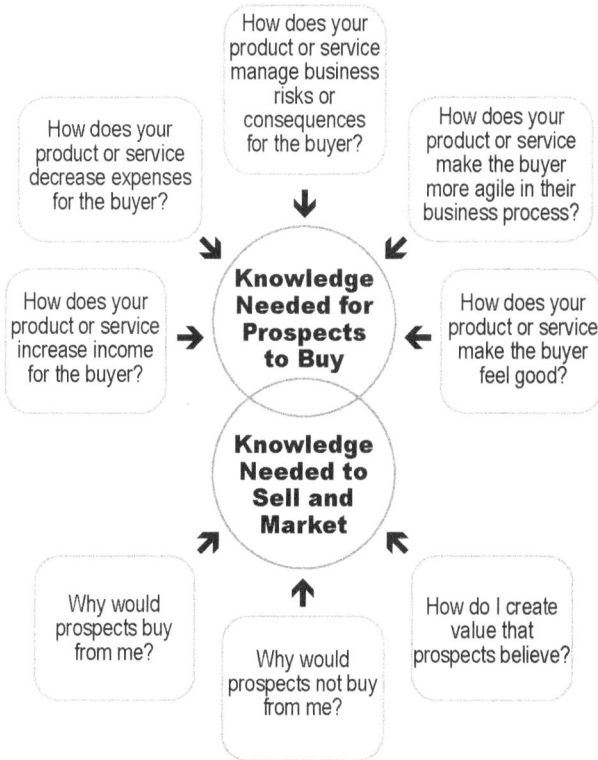

When these eight questions are collectively posed, probed, and answered accurately, they create a unique demographic profile and operational blueprint of who your current targeted buyer is, why they buy or don't buy, and who your future buyer could be.

Additionally, when building your corporate strategy, these answers will help you manage your organizational design risks to help you maximize your strategy-perspective key performance indicators, and minimize wasted investments.

Strategy development is a multi-department layered process.

PEST Analysis

Another toolset needed to create and align corporate strategy, both with your growth objectives as well as with the other perspectives of the Revenue Capture Scorecard, is through the use of a PEST analysis. PEST is an acronym for Political, Economic, Social and Technology environment drivers that affect your current business model and your future growth objectives.

Strategy, like all scorecard perspectives, does not reside or operate in a vacuum. When developing your operational strategy for success, multiple PEST variables must be identified, forecasted, and addressed. Each one of these drivers can add or subtract from your stated corporate strategy and must be analyzed on how they affect your targeted buyer within the buying environment or geography that they operate in. Your strategy, both present and future, must assess these drivers on its formulation and execution capabilities to add greater understanding of why your strategy execution will succeed or fail.

To increase your strategic perspective design success use a PEST model approach. By implementing a PEST analysis, you can assess these business model inhibitors to determine their potential impact.

Here are some common PEST areas to review when assessing their impact on your strategy creation:

Political Strategy Drivers
- Political party in power
- Government taxes
- Government regulations
- Government openness to international trade
- International Operational Stability
- War

Economic Strategy Drivers
- Employment / Unemployment
- Taxation
- Inflation
- Government and Business Debt

Social Strategy Drivers

- Education Stratification
- Health Stratification
- Welfare Stratification

Technology Strategy Drivers

- Cost
- Mobility
- Distribution and Accessibility
- Ease of Use
- Business Model Integration

To be effective and precise, and to minimize failure and maximize implementation execution, strategy creation should include an analysis of each these PEST factors for each business hypothesis you are considering.

Strategy Metrics to Measure

Like other perspectives, strategy needs to be measured and analyzed so key performance drivers can be adjusted to increase performance. One success-measurement for strategy (used by Google and Intel) is the **OKR** system. OKR stands for Outcomes and Key Results. This approach is focused on setting objectives and then measuring your success in reaching your goals.

The greater the clarity you have in your objectives, the easier it is for you to set up measurements that can be assigned. With clarity comes measurement, with measurement comes benchmarks that can be attained, and with benchmarks that can be attained comes growth that can be reached.

If you can't measure it, you can't manage it.

Here are some primary metrics to use in your strategy perspective of the Revenue Capture Scorecard to measure monthly.

1. **Market share penetration of sales opportunities.**

This metric measures your brand success selling in your market. It is defined as the percent of buyers who buy your brand within a stated time frame, divided by the target market size in the geography that you sell into.

2. **Quality control.**

This metric measures your product or service capabilities to a level of quality that is needed and the potential to maintain and achieve those standards.

3. **Client lifetime value measurement.**

Each client you sell has a revenue value that, in totality, can be measured over time through repeat purchases. This metric calculates their value to your organization.

4. **Vertical industry penetration.**

This metric measures your revenue capture success and your firm's ability to isolate buyer types within a selected market.

5. **Corporate profitability goal measurement.**

This metric identifies your product or service profitability against your corporate objectives.

6. **Operational efficiency measurement.**

This metric identifies your firm's operational performance and productivity for services delivered, products produced, and staff implemented against its total capability potential.

7. **Total sales measurement.**

This measures your company's total sales capture capabilities as compared to your company's stated corporate sales capture objective.

Chapter 4

Marketing Perspective

"Price is what you pay; value is what you get."
--Warren Buffet

Defining and Measuring the Marketing Perspective

Once you have identified your strategy perspective, you then need to build the marketing perspective link in your Revenue Capture Scorecard. The marketing perspective of the Revenue Capture Scorecard is focused on identifying and managing the marketing department's success contributions and costs to the company's revenue objectives.

Marketing, when managed and measured appropriately, provides the lead-generation engine to the sales team and your automated sales process to identify prospect opportunities that can create revenue. The marketing department can be a key business driver to corporate growth—but if managed incorrectly, it can reduce revenue capture, elongate the sales cycle, waste department funding, reduce inbound lead generation, reduce corporate cash flow, commoditize prospect offerings, and distract from an organization's capacity to reach its performance objectives.

Before you can measure and align marketing in the Revenue Capture Scorecard, you need to build a framework of distinction on what marketing is. Second, the success in managing the marketing perspective of your scorecard is also dependent on the interrelationship and accountability linkage it has with the other perspectives and the marketing department's ability to measure its ROI.

There are many strategic theorems and contradictions on what the definition of marketing is and what marketing's investments should do or produce.

Marketing, like the other Revenue Capture Scorecard perspectives, does not operate within a secluded environment. If sales team members incorrectly manage (or sell) qualified leads, it will drive down the marketing ROI calculations and unbalance your firm's capacity to hit its assigned revenue-capture goals and KPIs.

Marketing measurement is a premeditated process that integrates marketing analytics and marketing return-on-investment techniques and strategies to increase marketing success probability. When you formulate a foundation for marketing perspective success, there are critical operational questions that must be explored with applied research … and answered.

- Is your current marketing successful?

- How do you define marketing-expenditure success?

- Do you measure your marketing?

- Do you have a lead-generation tracking and scoring system integrated into your marketing department's programs to maximize your marketing expenditure and to track sales success?

- Have you built a written framework of your marketing objectives and the programs and investments needed for them to be successful?

- Do you calculate ROI for each marketing program you invest in and implement?

- Do you track key business drivers that define your success for each marketing program you implement?

- Is your chief marketing executive paid based on marketing ROI and KPI success?

How to Use Marketing and Return-on-Investment Calculations to Cost Effectively Turn Prospects Into Buyers

The key to success in marketing is not being the first to market, but rather being smart to market. *Smart marketing* is focused on measuring the value of your marketing investments and tracking the metrics needed to support those investments.

Marketing metric management is a premeditated process that integrates marketing analytics, marketing return-on-investment techniques, and thought-leadership strategies to increase marketing success.

I believe that marketing without ROI is wasted funding. When marketing analytics are combined with ROI and thought-leadership positioning is tied to the Revenue Capture Scorecard as an integrated perspective, companies maximize their marketing.

- Is your current marketing successful?
- Do your prospects believe your marketing?
- Do you know why prospects should buy from you?

- Is your marketing about you or about your buyers' needs?

All of these questions are action drivers that can be measured to make your marketing work.

All prospects are buyers at some time. Their buying cycle might be two minutes, two days, two weeks or two years—but at some point, if demand is greater than supply, prospects will buy.

To increase your marketing ROI, put your value up front so your prospects can turn themselves into buyers.

When buyers take action steps on their own to buy, they shorten their sales cycle timeline, eliminate competitive purchase options quickly, and determine a framework of how much they will spend (based on how they perceive your offering will hit one of their primary acquisition drivers).

By implementing a Revenue Capture Scorecard using marketing as a perspective, you will discover strategic and tactical action steps you can take to increase your marketing ROI, reduce your marketing budget, increase qualified inbound leads, and position yourself as a thought leader.

The Goal of Marketing

The simple goal of marketing is to create inbound leads that generate revenue.

Branding programs, positioning strategies, social networks, direct-mail copywriting, research analysts' reviews, public relations (commonly known as PR) in trade and business publications, attendance at tradeshows, print advertising, and inside telemarketing are all marketing tools designed to create revenue. This revenue may also be generated by reviews you receive from research companies and in trade publications. Revenue may be generated by prospects finding your website through search engine optimization (SEO) or prospects responding to a direct sales piece you distributed nationally. But as stated before ...

> PR is not revenue.
>
> Branding is not revenue.
>
> Marketing is not revenue.
>
> *Revenue* is revenue.

If your marketing does not create revenue for your company, then it has failed.

The Goal of Branding

Oftentimes brand-development spending is disproportionate to marketing ROI. Marketing managers invest in brand development without tying the investment to increased revenue capture.

CEOs want to know the ROI for their marketing dollars. Fuzzy marketing concepts that do not have revenue-capture streams identified with their approaches, like brand identity, building long-term relationships, and brand awareness, are developed by marketing executives who don't understand the most basic necessity: CEOs want marketing ROI.

If you can't link revenue generation directly or indirectly to your marketing program following its deployment, you are wasting your company's investment.

Is branding important? Yes, of course it is! Branding helps increase awareness during your sales cycle. Prospects that "know" you are more apt to buy from you if their perception of your brand fits their buying needs.

But brand investments must be linked directly or indirectly to prospect purchases. If you cannot link your marketing and brand programs to increased revenue, you might as well reduce your marketing budget, hire more salespeople, and/or increase your online presence and let your salespeople hunt for new business on their own.

Brand identification does not equate to brand acquisition.

Let's look at two of the most recognized brands in the world today: Microsoft and Coke. Both corporations have spent billions of dollars on brand development, brand communication, and brand maintenance—yet both companies' organic sales growth for new business is minimal.

All of us have bought a product or service that was higher priced than what we had budgeted—some unique offering that we did not research and for which we paid full retail price. Why?

Because based on our understanding of the offering's brand, we believed its value.

How many times must a prospective buyer hear that your company is committed to quality customer service, or your firm is a 100%-satisfaction-centered organization, or your business success is driven by the need to establish long-term relationships before you understand this is really just testosterone branding?

The marketing model of positioning bravado, commonly used by many marketing departments, where companies say "we are the best" or "we are committed to the buyer," is an ineffective and outdated communication process that pushes companies into a position of commodity with their competitors and minimizes the ability to track and measure metrics.

Don't you think your competitors say they are dedicated to quality customer service and consistent customer care as well? Of course, they do.

Is it not just good business to treat your customers well?

That's the point.

When you sound like your competition and feed prospects grandiose platitudes about how great you are, you only end up burying your business value rather than putting it up front so prospects understand how you differ from the competition.

This traditional method of marketing forces you, your sales team, and your sales distribution models into a defensive position where you have to aggressively sell your value and position yourself against entrenched vendors, new competitors, and buyers who don't know how to buy correctly. This method of marketing increases your selling and marketing costs, extends your sales cycle length, reduces your inbound-lead generation and prospect purchases, decreases your average gross margin per sale, and minimizes your marketing ROI and ability to measure marketing metrics.

In a noisy marketplace, branding and value positioning often become intertwined as a singular concept that helps firms communicate who they are to prospects in a subtle and sometimes subliminal format. Yet, like all investments, this must be measured.

How a brand message is communicated and the action steps it induces prospects to take is the key linkage in business-to-business ROI justification.

Marketing to Buyers Who Do Not Know How to Buy Correctly

One mistake often made when developing marketing strategies is the belief that the targeted prospect knows how to buy your product or service. Prospects might know what they want or need—but that is not the same knowledge as knowing *how to buy*.

Assuming buyer knowledge based on the seniority of the title of the targeted prospect or on how often the prospect has actually bought your type of offering before will reduce your sales success. Realize it is not uncommon for "experienced buyers" to buy incorrectly over and over again.

And, when prospects make incorrect buying decisions, they might not have the funding to correct the wrong purchase for years; so they live with the mistake and you live with the lost revenue.

Never assume prospects know what they are doing, no matter their title or the verbose declarations they give you on how broad their experience level is in acquiring what you sell. To increase the communication and understanding of the value of what you sell, you must always assume that targeted prospects do not know how to buy what you sell.

To increase your buyer purchases, send a continuous flow of learning and thought-leadership communication devices through multiple media sources that force prospects to become educated while subliminally teaching them how to buy and what to buy from you.

To close any knowledge gap and tighten your marketing ROI, you must create detailed client questionnaires, assessments, and Q&A marketing material for your sales team and sales process to help gauge the buying knowledge of the prospect and to position your firm as a thought leader.

The better your buyers know how to correctly buy what you sell, the greater potential your marketing programs will have to induce buyers to take action steps toward purchasing from you—and the greater your marketing return on investment will be.

Metric Measurement Paradigm

Often the timeline of a company's sales cycle and their prospects' buying cycles are not the same; so sales and marketing teams struggle with their process and approach on how to close this buyer disconnect. The way to shorten prospects' buying cycles is through a continuous marketing engagement approach where prospects are educated on your offerings' value over and over again.

When prospects decide to buy from you based on their perception of your value, they eliminate competitors for you and call you when they are ready to buy, or go online to make a purchase, and minimize their own price resistance because they believe your value is equal to or greater than your price.

The fact is, most marketing programs are ineffective and lack ROI checks and balances because companies sound and act like their competitors and neglect to put their distinctive value in front of the buyer.

To turn prospects into active buyers, you must stop wasting budget dollars on beautiful four-color brochures that no one reads, multimedia presentations that may be visually attractive but do not say how your offering helps a business succeed, social media that is only about you, or press releases promulgating your new strategic partnership which conversely marked you as one of many versus one of one. These marketing devices are one dimensional and do not stimulate or enlighten buyers or induce them to buy.

One-dimensional sensory marketing puts prospects into sleep mode. When your marketing is one dimensional, it is too passive for the average prospect and creates lazy buyers who don't buy or who buy incorrectly.

Because consumers are daily overwhelmed by the various multimedia they are exposed to, it is critical you adopt a marketing model that deploys multisensory value communication to stimulate action steps and thought-leadership purchases.

The correct way to create buyer engagement with targeted buyers is to get them involved in the discovery of your value.

Value must be multisensory and multidimensional. Value identification must be driven by buyer participation.

When prospects feel they are buying and not being sold, they buy faster and more often.

To sell more and to create inbound leads for your sales team and your sales process, your marketing programs need to educate targeted buyers on how your product or service can help them and subliminally teach them how to buy correctly.

To sell more and to turn targeted prospects into customers, marketing must provide deep educational content.

Identify Your Buyer's Business Drivers To Increase Marketing ROI

Value identification and packaging is a complex and integrated process that requires market research, customer analysis, and assumptive observation. The more you understand your buyers' business drivers, the higher your marketing ROI is.

When creating a marketing program, there are direct and indirect drivers that must be identified and managed to maximize your buyers' multidimensional value acceptance.

Often, the value of what you market is misperceived by your targeted buyers. This value separation is called the "value variance." Because prospects' emotional and financial goals are attached to their needs, they see value from only one perspective, and that value can vary regardless of their title or position. To increase marketing success, you must close the value-variance gap.

Let's take a look at some questions that can help you assess how to close the value-variance gap for your offerings.

Assessing the Value-Variance Gap

1. Does your marketing discuss the quality of your offering's support as a key differentiation of why prospects should buy from you?

   Yes • No

2. When you lose a sale, do prospects communicate more than 50% of the time that your price was too high?

   Yes • No

3. Do you market your firm's products or services horizontally to everyone, or do you market vertically to specific markets with separate positioning?

   Horizontally • Vertically

4. Does your firm lead with price as its sales value proposition when marketing to a

prospect?

Yes • No

5. Is the word "price" mentioned anywhere in your advertising, including sales brochures and direct mail pieces, or on your website and social media sites?

Yes • No

6. In the final steps of the sales cycle to buy your offering, do prospects seek information from you on how you are different from your competitors more than 50% of the time?

Yes • No

7. Is your pricing metrics based on your competition's price?

Yes • No

8. On repeat sales to existing clients, do your customers hold you hostage for discounts to get add-on business?

Yes • No

9. Does your website's home page highlight how your offerings can help your prospects and describe specifically how you do this?

   Yes • No

10. Does your marketing communication emulate the marketing messages of your direct and indirect competitors?

    Yes • No

Correct Answers

1 – No	6 – No
2 – No	7 – No
3 – Vertically	8 – No
4 – No	9 – Yes
5 – No	10 – No

Scoring

Each correct answer is worth 10 points. Each incorrect answer receives 0 points. Add up your score.

80 and above: Your communicated value is reflective of the value seen by prospects.

60 to 80: A small value variance exists between what you believe your value to be and what your buyers may perceive to be your value.

50 and below: Your value variance is wide and does not correctly communicate why your prospects buy. This gap reduces your ability to understand how to successfully market to your targeted prospects.

To help package your value correctly and ultimately measure it, you need to identify what category of value your prospects use as a key driver for them to take an action step to buy.

Direct Value-Buyer Drivers

This is the most obvious value that prospects verbalize during the pre-purchase sales cycle or during market research programs as reasons why they will buy. This is not always an accurate or honest reason why someone buys, but usually it is the most visible during the pre-sale or pre-purchase process.

Direct value is often based on how your product or service delivers results to the buyer; so "value demonstration" in your marketing approach must be succinct.

Without understanding why your targeted prospects buy, it is hard to develop coherent marketing programs that communicate your value up front (or in any other fashion) that can be merged into your Revenue Capture Scorecard. To make your marketing program work, you must identify your buyers' action drivers. Action drivers are key reasons why your targeted prospects purchase. By understanding the reasons why your prospects buy, you can then craft value messages, branding positions, and buyer inducements based on their needs as buyers, not your needs as a seller.

In addition to the five primary drivers that make businesses buy (provided on page 30), there are also secondary indirect drivers that influence prospects to take action steps which you should consider.

Indirect Value-Buyer Drivers

Indirect value-buyer drivers can be stronger influencers than a direct-value declaration, but they are not always obvious or verbalized. Indirect value is often a buying driver laced with ego, psychological issues, physical issues, or risk management variables that must be taken into consideration to correctly increase your marketing success.

Remember, gaining an understanding of your business value, why your prospects buy, and who they are will improve marketing expenditure efficiency and ROI calculation.

Below I have identified eight indirect buyer drivers you should consider when developing your marketing program to help you maximize and measure your marketing effectiveness.

1. Change Value

Some prospects buy from a different vendor or seller to try someone or something new. They are just seeking change.

2. Human Capital Value

Human capital value is obtained when the purchased offering brings business value by helping buyers increase communication and interactivity between their employees, business partners, or customers.

3. Performance Value

Performance value increases the efficiency of the prospect's business or personal activities by improving business asset usage like machinery, facility, distribution system, etc., or their personal performance in a particular area.

4. Competitive Value

Competitive value is important to buyers seeking to reposition, adjust, or take over their market or improve their personal activities through the implementation of a purchase as a tool to create a disproportionate market or lifestyle advantage.

5. Launch Value

Launch value is achieved when the purchase of a service or product is used to help companies or individuals break into new markets or industries on an accelerated timeline.

6. Consequence-Management Value

Prospects are driven by fear or make purchases based on managing risk or consequences. This driver forces prospects to take action steps to buy, often regardless of budget limitations.

7. Family Value

Prospects are driven to buy based how on they believe the purchase will affect their families' comfort and safety. More than ego, family value is an emotional and psychological feeling they get when the purchase affects their life holistically.

8. Layered Value

Layered value is when more than two drivers (direct or indirect) are used by prospects to make buying decisions. Oftentimes, layered values are not obvious or communicated by the prospect; rather they are identified through in-depth conversations.

To increase your marketing return on investment and maximize your measurement capabilities, study these direct and indirect value-buyer drivers to determine which ones are present in the products and services you sell.

Keep in mind, your products and services may not produce these drivers directly for your prospects but rather indirectly through productivity improvement, better management reporting, increased staff knowledge, or life enhancement perceived by the buyer.

Examples of value-buyer drivers:

Product or Service	**Buyer Driver**
Life insurance	Risk management protection for family (family value)
Software	Reduce costs for business (decrease expenses value)
Wholesale jewelry	Increase inventory turns for retailer (increase income value)
Weight-loss pill	Make the buyer happy (feel good value)

With this data, you can craft marketing programs that position your value up front and hopefully can be measured.

Telling your targeted prospects about your offering's attributes and not the results your offering delivers at the beginning of your marketing delivery cycle (which foreshadows your selling process) will diminish your growth potential. Study these primary and secondary drivers and your offering's mix to determine what the specific drivers will be and how they can be communicated.

Marketing ROI

Historically, the marketing department has been a staff position in support of the line position of sales. Through this traditional relationship (depending on the size of the firm), the vice president of marketing or the senior marketing person reports to the Senior VP of Sales and Marketing or maybe a Chief Operating Officer (COO).

Most marketing managers have evolved from a traditional marketing and communications background that includes graphic design, press management, copywriting, tradeshow supervision, sales, and sometimes direct mail. In the digital economy, some managers even have B2B interactive experience (more common in B2C) with e-mail, e-zine, social networks, and webinars.

The Internet has become a critical selling medium that can produce sales transactions and qualified leads. Thus, expectations and compensation for marketing executives must be expanded to encompass the Web. With their increased responsibility, marketing managers need to be held accountable to a budgeted monthly revenue quota or sales forecast, just like the sales department with the same expected ROI.

The purpose of this integrated marketing program is to tie all senior managers directly to corporate revenue goals that are mutually managed by the department heads as a group quota. By elevating the status, responsibilities, and compensation of marketing management, you reinforce their partnership in revenue capture with the sales department, or your sales process, and the company as a whole.

Is this a new direction for most firms? Yes.

Is this the future for companies that seek to have an integrated outbound-revenue capture machine? Yes.

How do you accomplish this? First, you must determine how the marketing department will be held accountable to quantifiable revenue contribution and ROI.

In setting up your marketing department as a sales contributor to the corporate-revenue forecast, it is necessary to calculate the marketing department's costs to your firm by using a traditional ROI model. Start by looking at the cost of sales and the potential ROI, and then use this number as a benchmark against the investment in your marketing department and the potential ROI on that investment. To find this number, calculate the average cost of a salesperson. The following example is a rough calculation. Obviously, you will need to calculate costs from your own business model to determine an accurate ROI.

The average base salary (or draw versus commission) for salespeople in North America in our current economy ranges from $35,000 to $110,000 annually, depending on the industry. In this example, I will use $87,500.

Salary	$87,500
Commissions calculated at quota	$100,000
Total annual compensation	$187,500
Plus benefits, taxes, insurance at 30% of labor cost	$56,250
Cost including benefits and wages	$243,750
Travel and expenses calculated at $3,000/month	$36,000
Total salesperson's annual cost	$279,750

For this example, the salesperson has a $1,500,000 annual quota and the firm operates on a service/product margin of 45%

Sales	$1,500,000
Minus cost of goods	$825,000
Total gross margin	$675,000
Total gross margin contribution before corporate G&A	$675,000
Minus total salesperson costs	$279,750
Equals gross revenue contribution per salesperson before corporate G&A (General and Administrative) costs	$395,250

This example is an estimate only and does not calculate the cost of sales opportunities generated by the marketing department. This model assumes each salesperson will find, present, and close all of his or her lead generation.

Using this example, you should generate $395,250 in gross revenue contribution before corporate G&A, or a 141% return on your investment of $279,750 for the salesperson's cost.

With this number, you can now benchmark the marketing department's budget, with the assumption that it must return a minimum of 141% for every dollar invested.

Is this an accurate way to determine ROI for marketing projects? Yes and no.

In this example, the marketing department needs to understand that for every dollar they divert from the deployment of salespeople, or a sales process, they are potentially diverting a calculable 141% return on investment for the firm. Business-development spending is based on maximizing revenue opportunities. Marketing departments, like other departments, must realize that all spending is tied to ROI.

When determining a budget value, you need to calculate its ROI potential against the same or greater investment in sales.

Steps to Calculate Marketing ROI

1. Create or develop a twelve-month plan (month by month) listing each event or action the marketing department will take during the business fiscal year (i.e., January seminar, February direct mail, March eZine, April YouTube video, etc.).

2. Assign a fixed cost to each event based on the event's assigned budget.

3. Calculate the required ROI, in dollars, based on the event's contribution.

4. Verify that the project's ROI matches the ROI or higher that a salesperson's costs would contribute.

5. Make a business decision, i.e., is this an appropriate investment?

Measuring ROI

Marketing, to some degree, is the black hole that has never been held accountable to a measurable standard. As the position of marketing becomes more elevated, it is apparent that companies need to track the results of this department's actions as a business metric.

What kinds of metrics should you measure and what are their values?

Like our previous discussion, there is vagueness to some ROI calculations when determining marketing programs. But it behooves any senior management team to develop business measures.

The following can be directly measured in a price ratio:

- Direct mail
- Telemarketing
- Public seminars
- PR
- Webinars
- Print advertising
- Opt-in e-mail
- Social media
- eZines
- Tradeshows
- Internal marketing material
- Teleseminars
- Search engine optimization

For example, if the cost of a direct mail lead is $100 and it takes twenty-five qualified leads to close a sale, then your marketing costs are $2,500 per order plus your marketing department overhead.

Segment Your Market to Tighten ROI

When building a growth plan for your business, you must develop different marketing propositions for each geographical area that you market to. Prospects are not rigid, stone-like clones of each other. They have unique value-identification demands based on where they are located and who they are. Prospects in London, Tokyo, Boston, Chicago, and LA have different value-buyer drivers.

Geomarketing

Geomarketing is the sub-segmenting of prospects by geography and the traditional four Ps of marketing: Price, Promotion, Position, and Product relevant to geography.

Geomarketing can:

- Sub-segment opportunities within larger geographies (Atlanta within Georgia)

- Identify new markets to enter and expose market gaps

- Refine sales and marketing budget allocation

- Personalize your marketing messages based on geography

Use geomarketing to maximize marketing expenditures and ROI calculation based on isolating qualified prospects by location.

Spatial Marketing

Spatial marketing is an analysis tool used to study how buyers purchase based on their unique characteristics and the physical environments they operate in. Spatial marketing goes deeper than geomarketing by helping you analyze the intersection of buyer-value based on your offering's distribution capabilities and communication methods; your competitors; the buyer's lifestyle, family life, and financing capabilities; and even weather—all within the same buying zone.

Oftentimes CEOs believe they can replicate regional business success on a national or international level without any spatial-marketing research to confirm this. But by spatial analysis, CEOs can calculate the potential for ROI more accurately.

Your marketing should start by building value uniquely, not globally, based on the spatial buying characteristics of your prospective buyers. Second, analyze each market separately. Well-to-do retirees in a waterfront community may perceive value for the same offering differently than prospects that live in a Midwest farming community.

Spatial marketing can help you:

- Forecast demand

- Profile your customers

- Minimize marketing investment mistakes

- Increase customer satisfaction levels by understanding the demographic flow of complaints (who complains and why)

- Tighten your marketing ROI calculation

Use spatial and geomarketing segmentation methods as business tools to increase the ROI of your marketing programs and as a foundation to make premeditated business decisions based on logic, not emotion.

Measuring Your PR ROI

At its core, PR is vague. The idea of being held accountable quantitatively is a difficult concept for

68

most marketing and PR professionals to digest and accept. For many, PR is the art of schmoozing.

The fact is, most successful PR is done with a telephone and a black book of contacts—yet its success and failure can be measured.

Remember, it is not the PR that counts—it is the revenue and return on investment that PR can generate that you must focus on.

Traditional PR folks calculate ROI using industry terms like:

> *Content Analysis Review*
>
> *Audience Impression Management*
>
> *Focus Group Reviews*
>
> *Client and Prospect Surveys*

To track the ROI on your PR accurately, follow these guidelines:

1. Assign a dollar value to each qualified sales lead generated by your PR. If your firm knows its leads-to-proposal, proposal-to-close ratios, website prospect-to-customer conversion, and the value of your average sale, then you can calculate the dollar value of every qualified lead generated. With this

value, calculate the total dollar value of all leads generated by your PR.

2. Assign a dollar value to having your firm's name or product and service published in a publication or third-party website. This is calculated by looking at the media kit of the publication to determine what they would charge you (before discount) for different types of advertising. If they get $12,000 for a full-page, four-color ad, and your PR has gotten you a two-page case study, then the PR is worth at least $24,000. If your press mention is proportionally smaller, then calculate the ROI based on a smaller ad. If you get your case study or firm mentioned on a business website, use the website's media kit to determine what the cost would be for a banner ad for the length of time your PR is kept on their site.

For example, if a B2B portal discusses your firm in a case study on its home page and leaves the article published for three days, calculate what it would cost for you to run a top banner ad on its site for three days.

Is this an accurate ROI calculation, since copy content has a greater market remembrance than advertising? No, but it is the minimum value of your PR ROI and will allow you to assign a dollar value to your PR successes.

"The aim of marketing is to know and understand the customer so well the product or service fits him and sells itself." --Peter Drucker

Measuring Your Brand ROI

Aggressively marketed and sold by ad and marketing agencies, branding is often the least-measured investment companies will make. Branding is often a soft, nebulous, and un-measureable marketing program that floats around a company's P&L and that never seems to go away.

Is branding important? Of course.

Is it measurable? Yes.

But brand recognition does not mean brand acquisition. Just because someone *knows* your company, product, or service *does not mean they will buy from you.*

Here is a simple and quick assessment you can use to quantify your brand marketing's value and its ROI calculation:

If you eliminated all of your direct, outbound marketing expenditures and any outside salespeople and sales distribution

71

channels, including wholesalers and distributors, would your customers visit your office, retail store, or website, or proactively call you on the phone and buy?

How much money does Apple spend on its advertising and branding as a percent of its total marketing budget? Yet, its customers line up and buy Apple's products.

Several years ago, I spoke at an annual conference for a national trucking association to a room full of CEOs about the concept of "Value First; Brand Second." During the Q&A period after my presentation, a CEO of a $100+ million family owned company that had been in business over thirty years, approached the audience microphone and said, "This all sounds great but we don't need to measure our strategy and metrics. We have been in business for so long, that we know every trucking need within a 100-mile radius of our corporate office and everyone knows us because our brand is so powerful." The room went quiet.

I asked him what his annual sales and marketing costs were per year and how many salespeople he employed. He responded he had about forty salespeople and his annual sales and marketing costs were about 10%, or $10 million, a year. I then asked him that if his brand was so powerful, why would he spend so much money trying to capture new business after thirty years—why didn't his customers just call and buy over the telephone?

He hesitated and said, "Maybe my brand isn't as strong as I think it is. Maybe I need to focus more on my metrics, to know what's going on."

And that's the point.

Oftentimes brand fatigue sets in. Brand fatigue happens when targeted prospects have been over-marketed on your business value and they do not believe your branding position and they don't buy anymore. At this point in their interaction with you, prospects have "matured" beyond your value and message declaration, reducing your revenue-capture success for new business from new prospects as well as new business from existing customers, thereby potentially increasing your sales and marketing costs.

New prospects are focused on your current branding message while existing customers and past customers go through a brand exhaustion where your message becomes irrelevant to their needs and they don't buy.

If your marketing (including branding) does not create revenue for your company, then it has failed.

Typically, brand-development spending is disproportionate to marketing ROI. Marketing management teams continually invest in brand management without tying these investments to increased revenue capture.

Branding is important, but it must drive corporate revenue success through linkage drivers that are identifiable.

If you cannot link your marketing and brand programs to increased revenue, you might as well reduce your marketing budget and hire more salespeople, or invest in more SEO or direct mail and let these investments hunt for new business for you.

As brilliantly discussed by W. Chan Kim and Renee Mauborgne in *Blue Ocean Strategy: How to Create Uncontested Market Space and Make Competition Irrelevant,* most companies lack true innovation and instead are just value and brand message repositions, up or down, of their market competitors. These "red ocean" firms do not create new demand in uncontested market spaces but instead just compete directly with established players in their industry. Most firms today use a red ocean marketing model that minimizes their lead generation, increases their sales and marketing costs, and reduces their ability to grow revenue organically using a scalable approach.

Thus, most marketing approaches within an identified marketing industry are only cloned copies of each other, adjusting their position up or down as it relates to their relative value position as compared to their perceived competitor's position and thus replicating a commodity-based marketing model that increases costs and minimizes ROI calculation.

Because of this cloned marketing process of "doing what your biggest competitor does," marketing programs today have become reactive, antiquated business models that ultimately fail because they do not communicate your company's value. This approach forces your company to pull its business value behind it, making it difficult for new prospects and existing customers to clearly see what your true business value is.

Additionally, small and medium-sized businesses emulate the marketing of large corporate competitors with the misperception that the large competitor has spent millions of dollars on research to support the marketing programs. On the surface, this seems like a reasonable assumption, but the fact is, large corporations spend the bulk of their research on the offering itself, not necessarily the marketing. There are many large companies that do not track their marketing ROI nor do they manage their marketing department by metrics.

Take a look at any small or large company's marketing materials, including their website, social media, corporate brochure, direct mail pieces, advertising, business proposals, and press releases and you will find the same corporate-value communication messages such as: "We are good at what we do." "We are customer centric." "We are innovative and different from the competition." "We are dedicated to our client's performance."

This reactive approach creates marketing communications that are distributed to prospects with the hope that they will take action steps to buy with no lead-scoring or targeted-buyer measurement. Unfortunately, this approach historically creates minimal inbound lead generation, or worse, creates unqualified leads that waste the sales staff's time or your marketing investment costs, and can't be cost justified.

When is the last time a prospect looked at your four-color, high-gloss, eight-page corporate brochure or went to your website and said, "Wow! This is amazing! Let's call the salesperson and buy now ... or let's get online and buy it immediately!"?

This reactive marketing approach is a recurring process, played over and over again in small, private companies, mature corporations, and Global 1000 players. Reactive marketing drives down a company's competitive strategy success and creates a high probability that its marketing ROI calculation will be low.

One way to increase marketing ROI integration success and build a metric model that can be measured in your Revenue Capture Scorecard is to focus your outbound-marketing programs on your firm's unique company's core competence capabilities that are based on your value—not your competitors'—and then to measure your lead generation against this investment.

As stated earlier, brand identification does not equate to brand acquisition, so brand management and marketing expenditure must use a framework that has a high probability of ROI calculation and measurement. When the metrics used by department executives are not measured accurately it affects the accuracy of your Revenue Capture Scorecard.

Marketing Metrics to Measure

When setting up the marketing metric perspective of your Revenue Capture Scorecard, there are many items that can be tracked and measured to help you maximize your business model success.

It is important that you establish a lead scoring system. Lead scoring uses a business process where each lead is ranked and scored based on its value in the sales cycle to the sales team and how the prospect interacted with a salesperson or your automated sales-capture process. The total score is used to determine how leads are managed and/or released to your sales team or sales process. Lead scoring is a key business driver to help you manage your Revenue Capture Scorecard and to maximize your marketing investment efficiency and media selection.

Depending on your strategic corporate objectives, you should seek *to track a minimum of five to seven metrics weekly or monthly* in your marketing department. When trying to calculate ROI costs for your metrics in a small company, you can include fully loaded department costs. In a larger firm, you may calculate these metrics as just isolated events and before corporate G&A costs.

Here are ten marketing metrics you can potentially track and use in your Revenue Capture Scorecard:

1. **Cost per marketing lead.**

This cost is calculated by dividing the marketing program costs by the number of leads generated.

2. **Number of leads needed to generate one customer.**

This measurement tracks your marketing investment success potential to produce qualified leads that convert to sales.

3. **Marketing cost per sale.**

This metric tracks the total marketing costs linked to one sale.

4. **Website customer conversion ratio (CCR).**

This measurement measures your website's ability to convert unique visitors to your website (on a daily, weekly, or monthly basis) to individual prospects or buyers. How many prospects visited your website and how many bought or signed up for more information?

5. **Number of qualified leads generated per month.**

This tracks total leads generated by all sources in one month.

6. **Cost per tradeshow (conference, seminar, event) attendee.**

This is calculated by taking your event's total costs and dividing it by the number of people who attended your event (or visited your booth).

7. **ROI per tradeshow (conference, seminar, webinar, event).**

This is determined by taking the total revenue generated from the event and dividing it by its costs.

8. **Leads generated by marketing media type.**

This metric analyzes marketing program investment success by type such as print ads, direct mail, or online ads.

9. **Revenue generated by buyer-demographic type (male, female, manufacturing industry, hospitality, CEOs, CFOs, over 50, etc.).**

This metric measures your marketing department's understanding of who your mostly likely buyer is and identifies marketing adjustments that may be needed in your value messaging based on the lead segmentation type.

10. **Revenue generated by marketing expenditure type.**

This measures total revenue generated over a time period (day, week, month, quarter) for new business from new prospects and new business from existing customers by type of marketing expense.

Chapter 5

Sales Perspective

Defining and Measuring the Sales Perspective

Good sales management can be described as "standing barefoot on a sharp samurai battle sword while juggling uncooked eggs over your head."

Managing the function of sales is not a simple process and measuring can be even more complex based on the online and offline sales process your business deploys. Sales management requires a full-time, dedicated, premeditated process that allows you to create replicable and scalable programs that can be maintained, expanded, and measured.

Business success is centered on sales and revenue capture. Product and service delivery, corporate customer care, and operation development are important; but without sufficient revenues for your firm to grow, their need is minimalized.

It is challenging to find quality salespeople and to implement a successful automated sales process. The people are out there—but more often than not, the sales account managers are hiding in the back cubicles of your competitor's office or your automated sales process does not execute well.

Where are the sales hunters who can make your sales team successful? Where are the sales management team members who can drive team performance by metrics? Where is the automated sales process that captures revenue?

Can you name all of the companies that were dominant players in your market over the last 10, 20, or 30 years?

Where are they today?

To be successful in managing the function of sales, you need to maximize the investment, measure your current sales team and sales process, and set a pattern of team management that will help you and future sales team members become more successful.

The State of Sales Management and Sales Team Effectiveness

For many companies, the mechanics of sales management and the measurement of the effectiveness of its sales team is currently stuck in a cyclic format that was developed before 1980: annual sales projections based on backroom conversations with unsubstantiated forecast logic; marketing departments that spend money rather than create qualified, inbound-lead generation for the sales team; and managers who make judgmental observations on new product and service offerings independent of what salespeople can sell or the buyer will buy.

Sales team effectiveness is defined as building a staged sales process where each prospect's sales step is delineated and managed to create a scalable process of premeditated actions that are taken holistically by your company to move the sales process forward.

While many industries continue to evolve their operational capabilities around the Internet and the digital economy, many executives continue to manage their companies based on antiquated sales management concepts carried over from the organizational structures of Global 1000 corporations or some business article they read in a

84

trade publication for their industry. In doing so, they stagnate the effectiveness of their sales force and the growth of their firms as they attempt to increase revenue with aging sales methodologies and minimal metric measurement.

How you manage sales needs to be examined. Salespeople and your sales process either costs you money or makes you money. That's it. There is no middle position.

Sales force and sales process effectiveness is also about hiring and managing the right team and building a sales model that tracks performance by metrics during the sales cycle, and working with your leadership team to develop long-term planning and revenue capture that can be measured and linked to a scorecard.

To grow your firm, your business competence will not be determined by the quality of the product or service you sell. Although both are important, there are many case studies of companies with great customer offerings that failed because their sales process was inferior.

Conversely, there are many companies today with products or services that are not competitive and yet their revenues are growing dramatically year-over-year because of their leadership team's ability to proactively manage their metrics and the sales process they have implemented.

You notice, I did not say because of their sales staff skills.

Many times in sales-driven companies, singular successful salespeople become the figureheads or a poster boy (or girl) as the prototype sales approach the company wants to duplicate. However, individual sales success is oftentimes an anomaly that cannot be repeated or scaled, and aligning your sales management model around one person's success is not the way to accelerate your company's growth.

Yes, understanding the strategic and tactical techniques and action steps used by the top salesperson in your firm is important, but you must make sure these learned observations can be replicated and measured.

Your goal in managing your Revenue Capture Scorecard sales perspective is to develop a sales process that is scalable and replicable and can be documented, so you can forecast revenues to management with some accuracy. This approach helps executives create a business environment where they can be held accountable for their department's key performance indicators.

Business success relies on productive sales management and a productive sales process, not the strength of the product or service you sell.

Even the term *sales management* has changed. Years ago, *sales management* was a term loosely used to identify a manager that supervised a salesperson. In many firms, the vice president (or manager) of sales lived or died by the success of monthly revenue plans that were forecast twelve months earlier. They were the heroes or the goats, depending on how the revenue numbers hit that month. This evaluation process was an immature method used to determine revenue success (or failure) in a firm.

Today, the sales management team includes the entire ecosystem of a sales process and all of the associated areas used to generate revenue.

Firms need to focus on the integration of all their revenue elements of management. When one singular department fails to contribute, it directly affects all corporate revenue opportunities. At that point, it is not the sales department's failure to generate revenue, it is the company's failure.

Developing a Sales Process That Can Be Measured

Developing a successful and replicable sales process that can be measured in a Revenue Capture Scorecard is another driver to grow your firm. Like six sigma models, the correct sales process should minimize and eliminate business errors that reduce your sales operational efficiencies and increase corporate profitability. Having corporate revenue success is not always the result of a proven sales process.

Successful sales processes and KPIs are business maps that can be used by a broad range of sales team members over and over again. They elevate the skills of average salespeople to a corporate minimum and simultaneously improve the sales-capture system, while helping senior salespeople expand their achievements.

Deploying and managing sales metrics is an integral part of successful management and sales force effectiveness. Sales processes driven by metrics allow you to:

- Integrate its measurement to other Revenue Capture Scorecard perspectives.

- Reduce your sales cycle time to close the deal.

88

- Build automated online sales processes.

- Reduce sales-capture costs per sale, including travel and expenses and marketing costs.

- Increase your sales team's success.

- Develop a training program based on factual sales needs.

- Increase your sales team retention.

- Increase the efficiencies of your operations, engineering, and R&D groups.

- Create scalable, learnable sales processes that can be trained.

- Build an online sales engine that is scalable.

Companies' sales processes generally fall into one of five categories:

1. A sales process based on other companies' business practices.

2. A sales process based on unsubstantiated sales successes.

3. A sales process based on one top salesperson's success or the selling

experiences of the founder or senior manager.

4. No written sales process exists.

5. An online sales process that is not measured or managed.

As firms try to grow their business, they continue to fall backward as they attempt to sell using incompatible sales models that don't work for them and hold back their growth success.

Each of these methods hinders your ability to manage salespeople and deploy a scalable and replicable sales process and reduces your ability to measure drivers that maximize revenue. The key to making your Revenue Capture Scorecard successful is validating that the Key Performance Indicators you use are accurate and relevant to your corporate objectives.

Let's take a closer look at how these different sales processes are evaluated.

A sales process based on other companies' business practices.

Many times, a company will look at the sales processes of its competitors, or those companies described in industry trade publications, as models to emulate. Executives assume that using this method of imitation will provide their company the same success as these other companies. Generally, this never works because each company's core competencies and product and service strengths and weaknesses are uniquely different. Additionally, the sales team competence and sales processes may not be the same. For example, having a $20 million company adjust its sales process to match that of a Fortune 1000 company usually fails because the sales process of a Fortune 1000 company is not designed for revenue capture; it is designed for discipline and control. Most of the time, individual company competencies are not transposable from one competitor to another.

A sales process based on unsubstantiated sales successes.

For a sales process to work, it must be based on substantiated and documented successful sales steps and buyer profiling.

A sales process based on one salesperson's success or the selling experiences of the founder or senior manager.

Just because one salesperson or the founder of the company has been successful selling the company's product or service, does not mean that their sales process is scalable or replicable for the average salesperson. Sales process, to be successful, must be transposable to the masses to scale.

No written sales process exists.

Many firms use a verbalized sales process or an implied sales process, rather than having a premeditated, documented selling process for their sales team.

An online sales process that is not measured or managed.

When a business has implemented an online sales process, it is important for that process to be measured, managed and capable of being replicated on an ongoing basis.

In many companies, sales methodology is a haphazard approach, where some sales processes work and others do not. As mentioned before, part of the reason this occurs is because many sales processes are carried over from company to company without consideration for size, product, service, brand strength, financial capabilities, sales force, or management team. This haphazard approach exists throughout the world, in big companies and small, start-ups and mature players.

Evaluating Your Current Approach to Sales

Instead of looking at sales process personalization based on the business needs of its targeted buyers, many times firms just ask each other internally what they need to do differently to change their current business outcome. Worse, they make observations about a competitor and try to parallel those sales methods.

You will generate more sales by personalizing your sales model based on your market, your firm's strengths and weaknesses, and especially your prospects' needs. A successful sales process is the sum of your corporate skills, an assessment of your firm's operational assets, and the needs of the buyer. You must adapt your sales process to the prospect's needs, not necessarily what works for another company.

Sales Process and Strategy Test

To help you analyze your current sales process from the Revenue Capture Scorecard perspective, answer the following questions:

1. When sales revenue per salesperson is down or when your company's revenue is down, does your firm just hire more salespeople or change its selling model?

   Yes • No

2. Have you changed your sales model or sales process during the last 24 months?

   Yes • No

3. Do you have a written, documented, step-by-step sales model detailing your firm's entire sales process from pre-sale to post-sale?

   Yes • No

4. When your firm discusses new sales methods, does it only consult with internal peers and management?

   Yes • No

5. Does your sales team get paid the same commission for business from existing clients as business from new prospects?

   Yes • No

6. Does your firm use the same sales model to sell to CFOs, CIOs, CEOs, and general managers as it does to sell to lower-level managers?

   Yes • No

7. Does your firm track closing ratios by prospect title?

   Yes • No

8. Is your sales forecast/closing ratio at least 75% accurate month to month?

   Yes • No

9. Is your service or product pricing reactive to your competitors?

   Yes • No

10. Do your salespeople and your online selling system generate at least 50 new prospects each week?

    Yes • No

11. Do you allow only senior executives to be considered as qualified buyers when calculating your sales forecasting value

(versus accepting all manager titles as valid in your sales forecast)?

Yes • No

12. Does your sales strategy require action steps be taken by a prospect in order to be considered a qualified buyer (versus the responsive step model, where you wait for the prospect to respond to your sales communication)?

Yes • No

13. Does your plan offer multiple price point options to make it easier for prospects to buy (versus seeking big-ticket sales opportunities driven by price)?

Yes • No

14. Has your firm forecast the market demand based on research for each product and service you sell (versus a forecast based on assuming there is a demand or a market study that is more than a year old)?

Yes • No

15. Does your firm have a sales model that provides ongoing sales training for your

team (versus a sales model where team members must educate themselves as they go)?

Yes • No

16. Are your firm's marketing efforts feature- or service-driven based on the superiority of your product or service (versus pain-driven based on the prospect's needs)?

Yes • No

17. Is your firm market-driven by trying to sell horizontally to all industries (versus vertical-driven where each product and service has an identified market, price, prospect type, business need, etc.)?

Yes • No

18. Does your marketing department supply ten new qualified leads each week to each sales rep?

Yes • No

19. Is your sales team having a difficult time increasing sales from existing clients?

Yes • No

20. Are your sales quotas the same for revenue generated from new prospects as they are from existing customers?

Yes • No

Correct Answers

1 – No	11 – Yes
2 – Yes	12 – Yes
3 – Yes	13 – Yes
4 – No	14 – Yes
5 – No	15 – Yes
6 – No	16 – No
7 – Yes	17 – No
8 – Yes	18 – Yes
9 – No	19 – No
10 – Yes	20 – No

Scoring

Each correct answer is worth 5%. How did you score? Is your score above 70%? If not, you may need a new sales process to increase revenue.

When developing a successful sales strategy, it is important to make sure that the strategy itself does not stand alone, but integrates into the corporate business plan with the appropriate execution steps. Having the right sales process strategy is the key to successful sales execution.

Sales strategy first.
Sales success second!

Sales strategy is not just a verbal commitment to execute. It is also a detailed, written guideline used by management and staff to correctly implement the business strategy based on a specific sales model and the goals and objectives of the executive team.

If your sales strategy is vague and not detailed enough, your sales execution will fail.

Since compensation plans of sales staff and management should be tied directly to their ability to hit sales quotas and assigned sales goals, the sales strategy must be consistent with the team's ability to implement the sales process based on detailed logic and selling guidelines.

Your sales team cannot implement a sales process if the strategic groundwork has not been carefully developed or does not match your firm's current operating business model needs, sales team capabilities, and delivery capabilities. A sales process cannot be based on management's forecasted hope. It must be based on researched strategic logic and detailed, documented action steps that are trainable.

The Foundation of Developing a Replicable and Scalable Sales Process

To develop a replicable, scalable sales process that works and can be measured with the majority of your sales team requires you to:

1. Understand why prospects buy from you.

2. Understand why you lose business.

3. Learn how to show "value" that prospects believe based on specific buying criteria.

4. Document your sales process step-by-step.

5. Quantify your prospect prototype based on specific buyer criteria.

6. Determine the fully loaded cost of one sale before corporate general and administrative (G&A) costs.

7. Develop your sales metric benchmarks for success.

8. Document your top-ten sales objections on why your buyers don't buy from you with structured corporate responses.

9. Train your sales team regularly; role-play often.

10. Make cold-calling by telephone and through social networks a requirement for salespeople, not a haphazard, postponed event.

11. Provide a market potential of at least 300 prospects per salesperson, per selling geography, or identify an online market gap where demand is greater than supply where you can build an online sales model capture program.

12. Develop sales quotas or goals that are accurate.

13. Evaluate salespeople on metrics, not emotion.

14. Use lost sales analysis as a business tool.

15. Document your online buyer's purchase steps to manage abandoned shopping cart opportunities.

16. Build an online sales-capture process that is measurable and manageable.

With this information, you can build a step-by-step sales process that is measurable, scalable, and replicable.

Determining Sales Goals

When trying to prototype your sales-process model, your current prospects might not be the targeted buyers your company is seeking to sell. At times, salespeople take the path of least resistance and sell to prospects they feel comfortable selling to, not necessarily those whom management wants them to sell.

To develop a structured sales process that works, you must measure the gap between your current sales model, your current prospect prototype, and your corporate selling goals and objectives. If there is no gap, then (and only then) you can develop a sales process that is systematically measureable.

If there is a gap between your current sales success and your sales prospects then you must reduce the gap to change your sales team's (or your sales process's) focus on the company's needs.

- Is your sales team selling to the targeted prospects you want them to sell?

- Does your sales team focus on the right prospect title?

- Is your sales team only selling to existing customers?

- Is your sales team selling the product or services you want them to sell?

With the data from these questions, you can develop and write your sales process.

Documenting Your Sales Process

Once you have prototyped the demographic profile of your most likely buyer and current sales model, you can integrate these two resources into a written sales process that helps your sales team understand the model and the expectations you have for them to generate revenue.

Your sales process is the framework and, by default, the blueprint from which you and your sales team operate. It should be in a written format. Once the sales process is documented, it should be used as a tool to teach and manage your sales team and to drive them to perform as you expect.

Your sales process must:

1. Describe who your targeted industries are and what their annual revenues are.

2. Identify the title of the targeted prospect.

3. Describe the products and services you expect your sales team to sell.

4. Describe the targeted average price or margin goals per sale for each product and service you sell (gross profit or gross margin).

5. Describe the anticipated sales objections the sales rep can expect to hear from each industry they sell to and from each prospect title they are expected to sell.

6. List each sales step expected for each product and service you sell, both online and offline, through-person, and through-distance selling.

7. List how your sales team and sales process must qualify prospects at each step to determine if they should continue working with the prospect.

8. Identify the anticipated length of time it should take to close a sale from beginning to end and between each sales step.

9. Identify sales metric benchmarks for success.

10. Determine the expectations of lead generation (i.e., cold calling, networking, marketing, etc.).

11. Describe when and how often the company will provide sales training or amend its sales process.

12. Describe the structure and framework of each sales step, whether it is online, offline, or in person or a combination of all.

13. Identify the business drivers previously mentioned that will make buyers take an action step to buy.

Once you have gathered this information, pull it all together in a document that you provide to your sales team, and as needed, to your management team. You should review the sales process twice a year (or as metric analysis implies) to make sure it is relevant to your current selling environment.

To maximize sales success, make sure your sales team has the motivation and expected behavior needed for revenue capture. Small changes in your team's cultural behavior and educational process can have a dramatic effect in sales and your revenue capture success.

Salespeople are business assets that must be invested in—but salespeople must also invest in themselves so they are psychologically committed.

7 Factors of Successful Salespeople

Revenue-capture success requires that you maximize your sales force's effectiveness.

During the last couple of years, through our free, weekly, business-success-strategy newsletter, we have surveyed thousands of salespeople about their sales quotas and assigned sales targets. The survey results indicate seven consistent factors of salespeople who hit their quotas on a regular basis:

1. They cold-call new prospects by telephone and through social networks on a regular basis.

2. They invest in their own sales training.

3. They sell business results, not features or functions.

4. They talk like the buyer not a vendor.

5. They accept that sales is their career rather than a waiting station until their next job.

6. They document their sales steps and know their personal metrics.

7. They role-play on a monthly basis as part of their personal training process.

Evaluating Your Sales Team's Performance

Evaluating your sales team's successes and failures from a metric point of view is as important as the theoretical perception of what you need to do to hit your firm's sales forecasts based on the understanding of your market.

Anyone who has ever managed a sales team knows that sales quota success is not just tied to the team's selling skills, but is also influenced by how your firm markets and positions its products and services.

Having a sales strategy is good, but having a sales execution plan is better!

Understanding the business metrics of your firm's sales team is one of the keys to increasing sales and linking these metrics to other scorecard perspectives.

In many ways, managing a sales team is a mathematical model.

With data, you can slice and dice your sales team's analysis and make appropriate adjustments in training, employment, product and service pricing, and market growth opportunities. You can also use data to make rational and fair business decisions on individual team member's ability to sell under changing sales metrics.

Henry Clay once said, "Statistics are no substitute for judgment." By using both good sales statistics and sound judgment, you can sell more and know why.

Remember, the salesperson's paradigm: The buying cycle and selling cycle are never the same. So, using metrics (and a Revenue Capture Scorecard) will help you manage this vortex better.

Here are seven reasons most firms miss their projected revenue goals:

1. Failure to use an outbound-sales model to sell;
2. Lack of having a defined sales process that is replicable and scalable;
3. Continued calculation of inaccurate sales forecasts;
4. Continued confusion of what the company's business value really is … as determined by their prospects;
5. Continued deployment of relationship marketing as a revenue-generating approach for new prospects;

6. Failure to calculate market demand and reliance on the assumption that it exists; and

7. Failure to integrate strategy, marketing, and sales into one revenue-capture program.

Sales Metrics to Measure

If you have been involved in executive management for any period of time, you know that managing salespeople can be difficult. One objective, non-emotional way to manage salespeople is to use sales metrics that can be measured. Metric management is a tool that allows you to numerically measure salespeople to help align their action steps with your sales success expectations inside your Revenue Capture Scorecard. Sales metrics also help you understand the skillsets of each of your team members and develop training to fill any gaps in staff knowledge.

There are many metrics you can use to manage salespeople. Here are the major sales metrics that should be managed on a weekly or monthly basis for you to understand your sales team's effectiveness and training requirements. All of these can be measured on a weekly basis, but where appropriate, I have indicated when they can be measured monthly.

1. **Sales closing ratio by prospect title.** (*Monthly*)

This metric measures your account managers' sales success in selling your product or service to specific titles (i.e., sales success to CFOs versus sales success to VPs of Operations).

2. **Average discount off submitted proposal price.** (*Monthly*)

This metric tracks the average price range each salesperson sells at and their ability to sell larger deals. It also measures their ability not to discount off current corporate pricing guidelines.

3. **Average discount off submitted proposal price by buyer's title.** (*Monthly*)

This metric tracks individual sales staff success in selling to certain executive titles, such as vice presidents, or chief operating officers.

4. **Sales (in dollars) for each product and service sold per account sales manager.** (*Monthly*)

This metric tracks your sales team's focus on what specific product and service they like to sell and the success in dollars by offering type.

5. **Percent of closing ratio by product and service. (*Weekly*)**

This measures your account managers' sales success by product and service and number of separate deals sold per category.

6. **Percent of closing ratio by industry vertical. (*Monthly*)**

This metric tracks sales account managers' success by each industry they pursue to determine if there is a market focus imbalance (i.e., they prefer selling manufacturing instead of healthcare).

7. **Average length of sales cycle (from lead to signed contract) in weeks for each product and service account managers sell. (*Monthly*)**

This metric measures the average sales time for each account manager for each product and service they sell and helps sales management monitor sales forecasts for accuracies.

8. **Cold calls by telephone and through social networks made per day to new prospects. (*Weekly*)**

This metric measures how much a salesperson fills in the sales pipeline with opportunities from new prospects and also helps determine whether the salesperson is a Hunter or a Farmer.

9. **Cold calls made per day to existing customers.** (*Weekly*)

This metric measures how much your salesperson fills in the sales pipeline with opportunities from existing customers and also helps determine whether the salesperson is a Hunter or a Farmer.

10. **The number of leads it takes to get one sale.** (*Monthly*)

This metric tracks your ROI for marketing investment on a cost-per-lead basis. This metric also helps identify if a particular sales account manager requires more leads than other account managers, and vice versa.

11. **Overall closing ratios for all proposals submitted.** (*Monthly*)

This metric measures your sales staff's overall success as a percent of proposals submitted.

12. **Size of sales forecasts for each account manager based on individual closing ratios.** (*Monthly*)

This measurement tracks the potential for your sales staff to hit its sales forecast based on individual closing ratios. For example, if a sales rep's quota is $1,000,000 per year and she has a 25% closing ratio for proposals submitted, then she needs $4,000,000 in proposals in her sales forecast to hit her quota.

13. **Separate all sales staff into two categories (1) those with more than three years of experience in your firm and (2) those with less than three years of experience. Evaluate each against the peers in the same category. (*Monthly*)**

This measurement will help you individually evaluate and compare salespeople with their peers. Comparing a ten-year sales veteran in your firm against a two-year sales veteran in your firm is not a balanced approach.

14. **Number of first appointments made per month with qualified prospects. (*Monthly*)**

This metric measures your sales team's month-to-month effectiveness on getting new appointments.

15. **Number of second meetings, executive briefings, or demos completed per month with qualified prospects. (*Monthly*)**

This metric measures your sales team's month-to-month effectiveness on moving prospects forward to the next sales step.

16. Lost sales by type of sales objection. (*Monthly*)

This metric measures the impact specific sales objections have on closing deals.

17. Discount percentage by title sold. (*Monthly*)

This metric measures the negotiating skill your team has with specific business titles.

18. Discount percentage by business industry sold. (*Monthly*)

This metric measures industry profitability for your product or service.

19. Overall closing ratio by deal dollar size. (*Monthly*)

This metric measures the salesperson's negotiating skills based on the value of the deal.

20. Leads generated by networking. (*Monthly*)

This metric quantifies networking value.

21. Leads generated by marketing.

This metric measures the return on marketing investments.

A sales strategy without an execution plan is like a boat without a paddle: you can see the horizon, but you just can't get there from where you are at.

Chapter 6

Financial Management Perspective

Defining and Measuring the Financial Management Perspective

Financial metrics and models are the foundational infrastructure of all successful businesses. But, as a sub-segment of traditional financial metric measurement, there are specific KPIs and success calculations that need to be monitored to help accelerate revenue capture.

Early in my career, I worked as a vice president of operations for a technology Value Added Reseller (VAR) with about 300 employees. The company was metrically driven and each week our CFO produced a 100-page, estimated financial profit and loss statement for every department that showed line-item detail both before and after corporate

G&A. This detailed document was submitted to the executive team on Friday afternoon for weekend analysis and Monday morning discussion. Two weeks after the month closed, all estimated P&Ls were finalized for another review and assessment. The CFO in this firm was my mentor and instilled in me an operational efficiency mentality to continuously look at all parts of a business and break them down into sub-segment measurements.

The Role of Financial Executives in Driving Business Growth

I once had a CFO tell me, "Revenue improvement cures all." Yes, but it is also true that money can hide mistakes.

Revenue capture must be a coordinated approach. When attempting to build a business model that is scalable and replicable, the executive management team must concentrate on integrating departments, collecting metrics, and implementing best practices and a planned process.

Financial executives need to be proactive senior executives that drive other department heads (operations, sales, marketing) to greater metric-driven accountability for their department's performance and best practice implementations.

As stated before, no business department operates in a vacuum, especially when it comes to your business's financial metrics.

Accurate monthly sales forecasting is the key metric for a financial perspective to be successful.

Sales forecasting accuracy should be 75% or higher on a monthly basis. Businesses often function as an assembly line—with multiple moving components working in tandem to facilitate the production of a product or service that can be sold. The execution of installation, training, bench utilization, product production, inventory replenishment, software development, and marketing are symbiotic to the accuracy of the sales forecast. When the sales forecast is not accurate, the rest of the machine has to adjust its departmental execution. When sales forecasts are wrong, companies have to adjust their cash-flow projections, asset investments, marketing expenditures, labor allocation for projects, asset investments, new-hire timelines and potentially corporate G&A costs.

Many sales executives believe that sales forecasts are not viable business metrics that can be measured on a monthly basis due to the complexity of sales, but this is incorrect. All sales, regardless of their average sales-cycle timeline (from one day to two years) have specific process indicators that can be aligned to determine the forecast accuracy of a given sales purchase. The key to building an accurate sales prediction of when a client will buy is having a clear line of demarcation between the definition of what a sales forecast and sales pipeline are. **Sales forecasts** should only include sales opportunities that will be received as a signed agreement or a completed transaction in the corporate office within any 90-day period. All other prospect opportunities should be defined as a **sales pipeline**.

Sales forecasts are living, breathing snapshots of time that are always changing. Prospects fall in and out of pipeline and forecast positions depending on the changing variables that affect a sale (i.e., budget, decision-maker availability, competition). Yet often, sales team members and sales management want to include prospect opportunities that are complex, large-ticket deals with multiple decision makers and are more than 90 days out in their sales forecasts to validate their work effort. However, sales forecasts are not only sales team productivity assessments; they are also sales success measurements and operational tools for the entire company.

When sales leadership submits a monthly sales forecast, it should reach a minimum of 75% accuracy from projection to close. Anything less is an inaccurate calculation based on hope rather than reality.

For executive management to correctly manage revenue-capture metrics for the company, sales forecasts and operating costs must be accurate.

Sales Quotas Should Be Calculated Mathematically

Calculating accurate sales team member quotas is critical for your firm to succeed. By implementing a sales quota based on market research, market gap size, and definable business sales metrics, you can manage your firm profitably, satisfy your investor and funding sources, fund your growth, and capture sales at a lower cost. When incorrectly calculated (based on guesswork or industry estimates), your firm can fail.

There are ten sales quota calculation methods currently in use. These methods, supplied by multiple executives, use various foundations to determine assigned numbers. They include:

1. Using last year's territory sales numbers for this year's calculation model.

2. Cost of the salesperson times a multiplier (sales costs x 3).

3. Cost of corporate General Administrative (G&A) plus a gross margin.

4. Revenue goals committed to Wall Street or investors.

5. Total of the sales department's goals divided by the number of salespeople.

6. The salesperson's success the previous year.

7. An imaginary compensation number that was sold to the salesperson as his/her income potential if he/she hit 100% quota.

8. What the trade press says is the annual growth rate this year (up 12%, quotas are up 12%).

9. The VP of Sales' experiences at other companies.

10. A percentage of what the top salesperson did in his/her territory.

The above ten techniques represent the vast majority of sales calculation methods used today—and all of them are wrong.

These impractical and unscientific quota-determination methods are used over and over in both public and private firms. More often than not, the sales quota number is created based on commitments to investors, bankers, or Wall Street, combined with the perception of accounting regarding what the cost of sales should be.

The short-term losers are the sales reps as they struggle to make their monthly numbers. The long-term losers are the companies and their operating departments because business models have been budgeted on these inaccurate sales quota calculations. What do these measurements have to do with the potential of a particular salesperson's territory or assigned sales objective? These quotas are based on outside influences and expenses unrelated to the sales potential of the salesperson's product or service in an assigned territory.

When these quota determination models are used, more times than not, they only frustrate everyone. The Operations Department is upset because its bench utilization is low and management is forced to reduce payroll. The Accounting Department is upset because the company's business budgets are inaccurate which causes operating expenses to be disproportionate to forecasted corporate revenues. The Sales Department is frustrated because it can't hit its targeted numbers and no one is making his/her commissions. Investors and stockholders become disenchanted, lowering their commitment to your senior management team.

How to Calculate Sales Quotas

Here is a mathematical sales quota calculation formula that finance executives can use:

Sales Quota = territory potential (geography the salesperson sells in)

Divided by your firm's average sale (or specific product or service) in dollars

Divided by number of leads needed to generate one proposal

Multiplied by the average closing ratio of the sales team

Multiplied by the average value in dollars of one deal

This mathematical model provides an operating foundation to determine a target number for each sales territory that can be rolled into a national number and can be massaged and adjusted as needed based on an individual sales team member's performance, sales team goals, and corporate objectives.

Is this mathematical model a panacea to give each salesperson the most accurate sales quota that will measure his/her skill efficiency and forecast revenue capabilities exactly? No, but it is a metric-driven starting point for the finance department to work with sales management to calculate what the assigned sales quota should be.

New Sales Growth Ratio Calculation Metric

Often revenue improvement hides business model weaknesses. Rising revenues can often be segmented into categories of revenue increases, so gross revenue improvement does not always truly reflect overall business success. To accurately assess a firm's growth success potential, one metric you must measure is the net new sales growth ratio.

The net new sales growth ratio is calculated by counting in units the number of existing customers you have at the beginning of your fiscal year, adding any new customers in units you have sold by the end of that fiscal year, and subtracting in units any customers lost during the same timeline (i.e., existing customers, plus new customers, minus lost customers).

This metric gives you a definitive measurement of your firm's ability to organically capture new business from new prospects and your company's current capacity to maintain existing customer satisfaction at high levels. If you are losing in units (customers) more than you are selling in units, it identifies business areas that need correction.

124

Cash Management Through Sales-Cycle Selling Time Metric

For growth-directed firms, cash and revenue recognition are financial operating models that must be managed tightly to help facilitate appropriate governance and operational funding. One subliminal cash-management driver that can be improved and monitored is the sales team's sales-cycle selling time.

Calculating and managing the sales team's average prospect selling time helps forecast accurate cash-flow projections, improves revenue-recognition dates, and helps accelerate top-line revenue growth.

Selling is a time-management business model.

Growth-directed companies need to manage product and service sales as an inventory turn business, much like a retail store. The more inventory (unit sales) and staff placement (labor utilization) you can sell (turn inventory) within a fiscal year, the higher your revenue will be. Finance executives need to help sales team members understand selling timelines from the first contact with a prospect to contract-signing date.

Once average timelines are identified, it should become a companywide, collaborative effort to shorten prospect buying cycles by 25%, through adjustments of your sales, marketing, and strategy techniques to potentially increase annual revenue correspondingly.

Financial Metrics to Measure

Listed here are specific Revenue Capture Scorecard metrics you can measure to help you maximize your financial perspective success. By tracking these metrics *monthly*, you should be able to manage your revenue capture success model by adjusting KPI goals as needed to hit your corporate goals.

1. **Sales forecast accuracy.**

Measures your sales-process capability to manage buyer drivers and understand your selling model.

2. **Sales quota success.**

Measures the estimation of your sales team's individual performances accurately, as compared to assigned goals.

3. **Gross margin/gross profit per sale.**

The difference between your revenue and the cost of your service or product production.

4. **Sales and marketing costs as a percentage of revenue.**

Monitors cost as a percentage of your total revenue and flags excessive variable expenses.

5. **Net new sales to existing customers as a percentage of revenue.**

Measures the percentage of business generated from new customers as compared to total revenue.

6. **Average customer discount.**

Measures average percentage discount off retail pricing given to buyers.

7. **Inventory turn or bench utilization rates.**

Measures labor or product operational use and consumption, and the efficiency of its use as compared to its availability.

8. **Revenue per employee.**

Measures annual revenue generated per employee.

9. **Payroll as a percentage of sales.**

This metric shows total payroll expense for the company as a percentage of sales.

10. Accounts receivable aging.

This number reflects the average length of time between credit sales and payment receipts. It is crucial to maintaining positive liquidity. The lower, the better.

11. Advertising percent to sales.

This metric shows advertising expense for the company as a percentage of sales.

12. Cost of marketing as a percentage of sales.

This measures the total percentage of marketing costs as compared to total sales.

Through strategic observation, measurement and management of these financial metrics, you can build a cohesive analysis in your Revenue Capture Scorecard to help maximize your business model success. Financial perspective success is all about details and the management of that knowledge as it happens.

Chapter 7

Implementing the Revenue Capture Scorecard

The world is experiencing a paradigm shift for business creation and ongoing growth. The opportunity for companies to expand is dependent on their ability to generate internal profits to fund expansion.

When you have an increasing demand for internal corporate cash, paired with an increasing demand for capital investments to grow your top-line revenue, you create a vortex where funding has exceeded business requirements. This vortex is forcing many companies to miss business milestones, established players to reduce fixed costs, and mature firms to sell assets. As companies miss their management teams, investor milestones, or Wall Street commitments, they reduce their business valuation and subordinate their ability to succeed and fund growth.

The crucial issue for growth-directed companies in today's economy is to meet predetermined revenue milestones on time and on budget.

In a world where increased revenue has become an executive mantra, turning business plan strategy into actionable steps that create revenue has become, for some, an albatross.

The key to success is to continually increase internal funding capabilities and help reduce dependence on third-party funding resources. For companies to expand, business units must quickly produce tangible sales results.

When revenues are down, cash flows are affected and business decisions are driven by cash availability not management goals.

The use of the Revenue Capture Scorecard is driving fundamental business changes. By creating identifiable Revenue Capture Scorecard tactical measurements for each of your team members and contributing departments, you can transform silo performance into group performance, and create a pattern for integrated sales-team performance.

Unlike other management models, the Revenue Capture Scorecard focuses on directed metrics to help companies maximize revenue.

It is important to understand that revenue generation is a cause-and-effect process. Revenue will be short without a market-driven product, services to sell, or appropriate positioning support. When there is a revenue shortfall, success will be minimized if the focus is placed on the sales department as the driver for the shortfall rather than identifying and fixing the primary problem.

The Revenue Capture Scorecard is a visual device used to view the integrated variables of revenue generation from all four perspectives. Additionally, by identifying all drivers needed to generate revenue and/or non-contributions as they happen, you can make adjustments to your revenue-capture process.

The Revenue Capture Scorecard is more than a projection. It is a working battle plan to create interdepartmental collaboration and linkage to achieve tactical revenue goals simultaneously. It links interdepartmental success to corporate success and corporate revenue. It makes a sales forecast the company's responsibility rather than only the sales team.

Using a Revenue Capture Scorecard, you link multiple departments' responsibilities to the creation of revenue. Using this approach, the firm's business assets are centralized on revenue development and all departments are linked to that performance. With this linkage, the scorecard provides clarity in its strategic and tactical goals.

Implementing the Revenue Capture Scorecard

Set up metrics for sales, marketing, strategy, and finance that can be tracked monthly, and if possible, weekly. Set up a color-coded system for each objective metric goal to be measured where green represents that the assigned metric or goal was accomplished, yellow represents that the metric is in transition, and red represents that the metric or goal has been missed.[1]

On Fridays if measured weekly (or the last week of the month if measured monthly), have all department managers submit a task status to an office administrator for input in the scorecard. On Monday, hold an executive meeting and discuss the scorecard measurements with all managers having them work together collectively to achieve the business plan milestones.

---

[1] *To download a color-coded example of the Scorecard, visit www.pauldimodica.com/scorecard/*

As an executive, focus first on the color-coded yellow and red categories annotated in the Scorecard. These highlight the inability for department managers to complete their job tasks based on available assets or skillset issues. Once the yellow designation areas are reviewed, move on to the red, and then the green sections to determine the next steps.

Usually the failure of one department to reach its assigned metric will cause a cascading effect on the other departments, inducing them to fail as well. When this occurs, it is a good learning opportunity and teaching moment for the department manager who missed their objectives to understand how their department's failure affected all of the other departments and the impact it had on reaching the company's overall objectives.

Having associates understand their weekly or monthly goals and interacting as a team based on written expectations will increase corporate morale and business resolution. The key for any company to succeed and meet the milestones of its investors and management team is for all departments to work together collaboratively to create revenue. In a market where many employees work fifty or more hours a week, the Revenue Capture Scorecard can be the vortex where strategy turns into action. By linking departments' performance as a group, you will increase milestone execution and simultaneously increase corporate revenue.

The Revenue Capture Scorecard is a visual graphic to help corporate management integrate company departments into one outbound revenue-capture program.

Integrating the Four Perspectives

The development and deployment of the Revenue Capture Scorecard program is directly dependent on the title of the person reading this book and the influence he or she has in the firm and with the senior management team.

There are two approaches to deploy this program. The first is through a best practice review and ROI basis, working with each department head to build consensus and revenue maximization. I'll refer to this approach as the **ROI Approach.** The second (and more preferred method) is to adjust your entire revenue program from a top-down approach to integrate the four perspectives (sales, marketing, strategy, and finance) as an integrated program. I'll refer to this approach as the **Top-Down Approach.**

In this book, I only focus on the Top-Down Approach because the ROI Approach is a sub-segment of the Top-Down Approach (and is implemented on a department-by-department basis by focusing on the ROI discussion and tools previously reviewed for each of the four perspectives) and the Top-Down Approach is more complex to implement.

To be honest, it is never easy for a company to deploy a corporate-wide revenue growth success program because of the existing inertia of the old methods and installed bureaucracy that may be present—but this is the future.

The entire company—not just the vice president of sales—is responsible for sales.

The art of generating corporate revenue is always challenging and needs to be adapted to the continuing business environment in which you operate.

By deploying the Revenue Capture Scorecard, you are seeking to introduce a new model for revenue integration, team collaboration, department linkage, and business model success where revenue capture becomes a planned process.

Steps For Implementing the Top-Down Approach

Step 1: Get executive sponsorship.

The CEO/President or senior executive in charge must be involved. Not having senior management sponsorship will only create dissention among the management team members involved and will cause the senior executive implementing this program to fail.

Can senior VPs of sales and marketing and the CFO implement this program by themselves? Yes, if the vice president of sales has direct staff that is responsible for marketing, and strategy, as well as the sales process.

Once you decide to implement the Revenue Capture Scorecard, you must commit wholeheartedly.

Like other executive initiatives, assign yourself an appropriate timeline. If you are in the middle of a fiscal year, you might want to implement the basic model in stages, in anticipation of complete integration when the fiscal year budgeting is being planned.

Be aware that this program is going to change how you forecast business, generate revenue, fund departments, and compensate team members. This will cause a BIG cultural change for all involved—so proceed slowly.

Step 2: Assign Revenue Capture Scorecard responsibilities to named individuals.

As stated before, in a traditional organizational environment, positions like strategy and marketing are staff positions that support line positions like sales. Many times these supporting positions report directly to the senior executive. This is a mistake. The vice president of sales is held accountable for revenue that at times is controlled by executives who hold staff positions that may make unintentional counter-revenue decisions based on how they are evaluated and paid. So, the first step is to turn all prospective management positions into LINE POSITIONS. This way, they are now accountable and allocated the same business respect for that accountability.

Should they still report to the senior sales executive? That is open for debate based on your company's current organizational and political structure, but they all need to report to the same person so there is group responsibility for revenue.

Step 3: Determine and assign goals or revenue quotas.

All sales, marketing, strategy, and finance executives should now have dollar goals. These individual goals will link all of them together into a collective decision process to generate revenue. All decisions by the departments will be tied to one question: "Will my actions generate short- or long-term revenue for the company?" Under this model, the vice president of sales can still hit or miss his/her quota, but now he/she will have supporting management executives reinforcing him/her in this effort.

Generating quotas or goals for all of the managers must be based on real-world calculations, not backroom magic. Since marketing, strategy, and finance executives are not generally used to having their income derived from a quota-based system, they need confidence in the potential attainment of the quota and comfort that their numbers are logical.

What should the revenue goal for the senior executive of marketing be? The pivotal questions are: "Should their goals be included in the company's total sales quota normally assigned to the vice president of sales?" or "Should their quotas be ADDED to the vice president of sales' quota for a new, higher group quota?"

Each method has value, but in a new business-growth program, it is better to have quotas serve as contributing parts of the entire vice president of sales' quota. Once your outbound-sales management perspective program has completed one fiscal year, then you should have each prospective manager's goal calculated as a separate total. This way, during your program launch year, your vice president of sales can still hit his/her goal, even if the other contributing managers fail.

1. First twelve months of the Revenue Capture Scorecard: the senior managers of marketing, strategy, and finance are assigned goals that are sub-segments of the vice president of sales' quota.

2. Second twelve months of the Revenue Capture Scorecard: each prospective manager has his/her own individual goals.

Step 4: Determine compensation.

Like the sales executives, the marketing, strategy, and finance executives should be paid a base salary and commissions (or bonuses) based on the goals they personally (or their departments) are responsible for. Their base salary (like most VPs of

Sales) should only be a percentage of their total compensation. Under the quota system of compensation, the executives in charge of marketing, strategy, operations, and strategic alliances need to make more. Should their compensation plan increase? Yes. Should their compensation plan increases be tied to revenue? Yes.

Step 5: Implement business controls.

Most department managers have profit-margin guidelines and cost-management responsibilities. Similarly, all department managers must have business controls inserted in their compensation plans so their business decisions are not only driven by revenue, but also driven by good business logic. You are not seeking revenue for the sake of revenue, but smart and profitable revenue.

Step 6: Document your process.

All revenue quotas, goals, compensation plans, and common control mechanisms for the management executives must be in writing.

Step 7: Assign tasks.

As compensation plans change, it is imperative that you develop specific task assignments for each department manager (marketing, product

140

development, etc.) to measure their goal successes. As reviewed previously, you need to measure each department's tasks in finite and ROI capability. This way, you eliminate vagueness and focus on direct actions they should take to generate revenue.

Step 8: Hold departments accountable and link them.

Once the Revenue Capture Scorecard is in place and operational, it now becomes a management success tool to hold all departments accountable and linked collectively to their business performance. With this system, you now have a visual tool (red, green, and yellow) that allows you and your team to proactively manage your revenue capture and its contributing drivers. With this data, you can now adjust, modify, and amend business tactics and strategies to help the company reach its stated goals and objectives.

The Revenue Capture Scorecard process is a change management business model adjustment that takes commitment, time, and effort by all participants. If there is pressure to continue to work under a traditional organizational structure that keeps line and staff positions separated, you will find tremendous pressure not to change. Additionally, managers who are being held accountable for revenue for the first time will not like this new structure and compensation model.

Calculating ROI, quota, and tactical tasks for strategy, sales, and marketing managers will be an involved, interactive, and cumbersome process. I recommend you use your CFO or vice president of finance with each of the managers as a mediator to collectively have them determine what a fair quota is. Getting a "green light" from the management team is required for the Revenue Capture Scorecard to work.

Here is an important point—if your firm does not adapt its business model to an integrated, outbound revenue-capture program, it will never reach its full revenue potential. Instead, its existing organizational structure of rigid demarcation between line and staff positions will reinforce dysfunctional business decisions and continue to waste funding on non-ROI validated expenses.

Six-Month Implementation Plan

The following plan is designed to help your firm develop and deploy a Revenue Capture Scorecard program from the Top-Down Approach, company-wide to help sales management increase its success. Using the outline for a six-month program, you can follow the recommendations and slowly build your business case and methodology to bring about corporate consensus between both the managers involved and the associated department heads. This timeline can be accelerated depending on your team's agility, objectives, and ability to execute.

Note: All department heads should be involved in all meetings of the Revenue Capture Scorecard, even when not noted.

Prior to Launching

Have your current business model holistically assessed in its success model and department best-practice and metric-management to create a benchmark to measure against.

Month One

- Meet with the executives in charge of strategy, finance, sales, and marketing to discuss the Revenue Capture Scorecard management concept. The executive team should be present to handle general conversations and to communicate why the firm needs to evolve toward this goal.

- Review your sales forecasting methods and determine the firm's true sales opportunities based on cumulative territory potentials.

- Ask the executives from strategy, finance, and marketing to develop a list of ten KPIs they think can be measured from a ROI and revenue-generation point of view.

- Have the CFO and/or vice president of finance set up appointments with all of the managers to help them calculate their return on investment KPIs.

- Ask the HR department to draft new job descriptions for each manager.

Month Two

- Hold a second group meeting with the executive team and the business development group to discuss last month's conversation and ongoing investigations.

- The strategy, finance, and marketing department managers submit ten metrics for ROI calculations they think can be measured; attach these metrics to a budgeted quota for the executive committee.

- The executive committee reviews the new job description drafts from HR.

Month Three

- All of the executives who are involved reconfirm that the revenue and department calculations are reasonable based on market potential approach.

- Determine the goal assignments for the strategy, finance, marketing, and sales departments. If you have done your due diligence, looking at ROI by department, these numbers will be reasonably accepted by the department heads.

- Once the goal assignments are determined, insert them into the drafts of the managers' new job description supplied by HR.

- Review the new job description drafts with each manager.

- Review with the CFO how the ROIs will be tracked and what paperwork the department heads need to submit in order to help with the calculations.

- Determine how the top perspective metrics data will be collected (automated or manually).

- Review the new compensation plans for the managers. New base salaries, bonuses and commission payouts should be postponed for 90 days while the program is launched to help confirm the measurement methodologies and to work out any snags.

- If there is going to be a new organizational structure reflecting the changes of staff executives to line executives, have the CEO send an e-mail to everyone in the company announcing the organizational changes and the associated business logic.

- Insert the metrics developed from your new quota assignment into your Revenue Capture Scorecard. Use the scorecard as a tool for all managers to align and measure their revenue generation and quota attainment.

Month Four

- The scorecard management team holds its first integrated revenue meeting to discuss issues and determine revenue projects for the week. The group makes a presentation to the executive team.

- The CEO reviews calculations for ROI to help determine effectiveness.

Month Five

- The scorecard team meets with HR and the executive team to finalize job descriptions.

- The prospective management team generates a weekly executive report on group revenue issues and revenue quotas met, and then submits a draft of the report to the executive committee for review.

- The executive committee and prospective management team meet to review all implementation issues and resolve any bottlenecks.

Month Six

- The scorecard team meets to generate another weekly executive report, and submits it to the executive committee.

- All job descriptions and goals are finalized and become approved programs for the department managers.

Following are questions that need to be answered by management prior to the start of the implementation process:

1. Will the scorecard team be a part of the executive committee, report to it, or report to the vice president of sales?

2. How long will the transition timeline be for the new compensation plan to take effect?

3. If the current sales forecasts are inaccurate and not based on a territory market potential capability, how will the executive committee assign a perceived fair quota to the business development management team?

4. What percentage of each manager's total compensation should be based on metric attainment?

5. Who is the executive sponsor of this program—the vice president of sales, CEO, COO, or the team itself?

Although revenue capture is complex, I can assure you that after implementing the Revenue Capture Scorecard program, your firm's revenue will grow proportionately to your team's commitment.

The faster you can integrate the entire company (or division) into a management program where all department heads work together as one synergistic group focused on revenue capture, the greater your success will be.

Chapter 8

Conclusion

Business success requires detailed minutia linked to strategic action and operational execution. The management of executing detail is not always the most interesting or exciting driver of business success—but it is often the foundation that causes some companies to succeed and others to fail.

Understanding the interrelationship between departments and how departments are linked will drive the business-model adjustments executive teams must make to hit their revenue-growth objectives. Likewise, failing to manage the relationships between departments will immediately expose your firm to revenue-capture limitations.

Small changes in business-model coordination can generate huge changes in revenue-capture capabilities.

Department linkage and metric management with planning and execution drives revenue. No department is a silo; revenue capture is a companywide responsibility—especially in this global and fast-paced market.

I hope you have enjoyed this business success structure I laid out for you. Use it and build a revenue capture model that will take you to your goals. If you would like to discuss working together to implement the Revenue Capture Scorecard, give me a call and let's chat about how I can help.

Strategy without execution is wasted thought.

Paul DiModica
pdimodica@valueforward.com
770-632-7647

About the Author

Paul DiModica is the Founder and CEO of the Value Forward Group, a high tech business growth acceleration firm that integrates marketing, financial management, organizational development design, strategy, operations and sales process into one outbound revenue capture program.

Value Forward works with start-ups, investor funded players, family-run businesses and public companies.

Prior to founding the Value Forward Group in 2001, Paul also founded, e4Speed, a technology managed services, staffing and software project development firm with 45+ employees now owned by a Fortune 1000 company. As a visionary in 1996, Paul also launched iInform, a hospitality automation firm that rented (SaaS) business intelligence (BI) information software to restaurant chains using a touch screen browser accessed through the POS system.

Prior to launching his own companies, Paul spent eighteen years working with CEOs in business start-ups, Inc. 500 firms and Fortune 1000 companies. He has held the positions of Vice President of Sales and Marketing, Vice President of Sales, Senior Vice President of Sales and Marketing, Vice President of Operations and Vice President Worldwide of Strategic Development for a $900 million public company, reporting directly to the CEO and the Board of Directors, evaluating the divisional presidents' performances.

Paul has been featured or interviewed by the *New York Times, Investors Daily, Fox News, Selling Power Magazine, Sales and Marketing Magazine, CIO Magazine, CFO Magazine, Entrepreneur Magazine, Training Magazine, Marketing Magazine, Transport Times, Computer World Magazine, Entrepreneur Radio, Chicago Tribune, The Cleveland Sunday Paper, Kansas City Small Business Monthly, The Manager's Intelligence Report, Agent's Sales Journal, Executive Travel Magazine, Wisconsin Professional Journal, Time Compression Technologies Magazine, Minorities and Women Magazine, Broker Agent News, World Fence News, Affluent Magazine, Value Added Partners, The Merchant Magazine, Pennsylvania Business Central Magazine*, and many others.

Glossary

Agility: The ability to change and adapt according to the environment. As used in this book, *agility* describes a business's ability to modify its business process to adapt to changing industry, technology, and consumer needs.

G&A: General and administrative costs; includes the day-to-day operating expenditures.

KPI: Key Performance Indicators; metrics that define and measure your organizational progress from where you are to where you want to be.

MBO: Management by Objective; measuring what you do today against what you did yesterday.

OKR: Outcomes and Key Results; This approach is focused on setting objectives and then measuring your success in reaching your goals.

ROI: Return on Investment; the revenue that is realized from an investment, such as a marketing campaign.

Sales Forecast: Data on sales progress which include sales opportunities that will be received as a signed agreement or a completed transaction in the corporate office within any 90-day period.

Sales Pipeline: Data on sales opportunities in which no signed agreement or completed transaction is expected within 90 days.

Sales Process: A documented process by which your sales team progresses through the sales cycle; includes documentation on each step of the sales cycle from pre-sale to post-sale.

Frequently Asked Questions

Q **Does the Revenue Capture Scorecard process work in all sized companies?**

Yes. If your firm is growth-directed and seeking to build a scalable, revenue-capture system, The Revenue Capture Scorecard will work; regardless if it is a start-up, mature family business, midsized industry leader, or a Global 1000 firm. However, for this model to work, it does require a committed effort by senior management to be open to change.

Q **Are there other departments/areas that can be added to the Revenue Capture Scorecard team to help increase its success?**

Sales, marketing, strategy, and finance are key performance drivers and directly related to revenue capture. Other departments, like operations and engineering, may indirectly contribute to revenue capture but are lag drivers in day-to-day sales improvement. Without revenue, you do not need operations.

Q **Once the Revenue Capture Scorecard system is implemented, how long will it take to see revenue capture results?**

Once all of the revenue capture departments are linked together, within 30 days of data reporting, you should start to accumulate information that can help you adjust your revenue-capture approach. Revenue capture is a living metric that is adjusted as needed based on the data. Within one quarter (90 days), your Revenue Capture Scorecard should feed you enough trend analysis so you can start to modify your business models and increase your revenue capture. Within six months, you should be able to change any business processes that are not working or supporting your revenue capture capabilities.

Q **Is the Revenue Capture Scorecard only designed for companies that are having trouble growing revenue and profits?**

No. Even companies that are growing geometrically and experiencing top-line revenue and profit acceleration need to manage their business process by metrics and planning. Often, in fast-growing businesses (or business units) money hides operational inefficiencies that during a downturn could cripple the company's profitability or cash flow. Sometimes companies improve revenue and profits due to operational anomalies that cannot be duplicated and may only be one-time events. Singular revenue-improvement drivers, like one customer being responsible for 75% of your sales, one salesperson being the dominant seller, or recurring contracts that automatically raise their prices every year with cost-of-living adjustments (COLA) can hide business model inadequacies and give executive management a false sense of success security.

Q How will the Revenue Capture Scorecard adjust my management team's responsibilities?

This system will improve your management team's leadership and execution capabilities by supplying factual data that can be used as the foundation of their business model decisions. By removing innuendo, assumptions, and aged research from the judgment process, their operational adjustments of their departments will be based on professional criteria, while being aligned with the company's objectives.

Q **How is the Revenue Capture Scorecard different from having my executive team compensated in totality on profits and revenue?**

When management teams are only paid on companywide revenues and profits, it limits their leadership capabilities on making decisions. Department success must be linked collaboratively to corporate goals, with all managers working in tandem to make decisions that are not focused only on their goals but also the company's objectives.

Q **Do you help with Revenue Capture Scorecard setup and business-model assessment?**

Yes. At the Value Forward Group, we work with clients in many capacities, including complete business-model success assessments and supplying written business-model changes and suggestions that we help clients implement. Once changes are completed, we then help clients create a Revenue Capture Scorecard.

Keynote Speaking, Conferences and Kick-Off Meetings

Have Paul DiModica speak at your next event!

Paul DiModica is a member of the National Speaker's Association (NSA) and speaks worldwide on high tech sales, marketing, strategy and leadership delivering motivational and content-rich presentations that help audiences understand how to increase their personal and corporate performance based on proven strategic and tactical actions they can take immediately. All programs are custom fitted to the client's needs and objectives and combine humor, actionable content and audience engagement.

Paul is available for keynote speaking, kick-off meetings, partner conferences, and company-wide learning. Performance topics include:

- How to Sell Management as a Peer Not a Vendor
- How to Create Value That Buyers Believe
- Leadership in 6 Words or Less

Call us today at (770) 632-7647 or visit www.PaulDiModica.com

High Tech CEO & Team Advisement Services

High Tech 360° Business Success Assessment and Recommendations Program

The Value Forward High Tech 360° Business Model Success and Recommendations Program is a compressive detailed program designed to help companies integrate financial management, marketing, strategy, operations and sales into one outbound revenue capture program. Through our program, we evaluate your business from your prospect's point of view, then from the management team's point of view, and then recommend specific detailed action steps to close the gap between how you see yourself and how prospects see you. Once these recommendations are made, we then work with you and you team in tandem to implement our suggestions.

Value Forward Guided Progress Success (GPS) System

The Value Forward GPS System is a 12-month planned business success program designed to give growth directed clients a step-by-step architectural blueprint to improve their firm's performance.

Using our three sequential stages of analyzing, strategizing and monetizing, we work with senior executives to help build a replicable and scalable revenue capture program based on their goals, their company's core competencies, and industry best practices. A detailed written list of action steps is provided and through a collaborative process, we work with the management team in tandem to execute changes to the business design and operational framework to maximize their corporate success.

IT Team Strategy, Marketing and Sales Training Success Workshops and Advisement Programs

At the Value Forward Group, we offer a broad range of programs and services designed to help sales and marketing teams grow their business revenue and build scalable and replicable revenue capture programs. Our sales training and strategy programs are designed to help you and your team "become a peer in the boardroom, instead of a vendor waiting in the hallway[®]." Through specific

Value Forward tactical techniques and methods, we teach you how to put your business value in front of you so your prospects see you as strategic advisor and take action steps to buy.

We can custom-fit our programs based on your business needs and objectives.

Call us today at (770) 632-7647
or visit www.PaulDiModica.com

Sign-up for Our Free Weekly IT Business Success Newsletter

HighTechSuccess
www.hightechsuccess.com

HighTechSuccess is designed for corporate executives in growth directed firms. It provides best practices, case studies and proven methods to increase high tech business success.